Tame Your Woman™
How to Become the Man She Needs

By Carl E. Stevens, Jr.

Self-As-Source Publishing

Tame Your Woman

FIRST EDITION

ISBN: 978-0-9801663-2-3

0-9801663-2-2

Published By: Self-As-Source Publishing

Web Address: http://www.jujumama.com
http://manifestsexy.com/

Cover Image: Marlene Hawthrone Thomas, Photographer
http://www.obsidianeyephoto.com/

Cover Design: Dunn + Associates
http://www.dunn-design.com/

Edited by: Aneesah Akram and Jason Corwin
Formatted by: Tanisha J. McClellan

Tame Your Woman

<u>Dedication</u>

To my wife and spiritual partner across lifetimes Kenya K. Stevens. You are a true light for the world and I love and honor you always.

To Senbi, Sanu, and Kaheri for being the bravest children I know.

To my father Alvin R. Emerson III for being the best example in my life and childhood of what being a man is all about.

To my mother Joann Emerson for loving me unconditionally and demonstrating what being a woman is all about.

To my brother John Stevens for upholding the masculine values of the Leader and Soldier in everything he does.

To my brother Chad Stevens for the support he has provided to me and our family over the years.

To Ayana Denise Johnson for being my greatest friend and for holding the spirit and vision for this book.

To Master Yao Nyamekye Morris for being my spiritual brother and always supporting our family.

Table of Contents

PREFACE

This book is intended for men who want a different perspective and approach for improving their relationships with the women they love. It provides a set of four *masculine principles* that improve our capacity to come into our character traits of the Monk – setting the proper direction for our families, the Leader – being present and accountable to our wives and loved ones, the Soldier – willing to sacrifice for others, and the Negotiator – improving the quality of our communication. Although these principles can offer the keys to an improved success rate in the way men relate with women, they are not meant to be perceived as catch-all solutions for every man.

Tame Your Woman's unique presentation is based upon the mathematical aspects of universal law. In other words, it explains the science of our inherent natures as masculine and feminine beings using the foundations and application of universal laws to define our responsibilities and approach to relationships as men. Universal laws are important because they can be applied to every aspect of our lives especially how we function in relationships.

I am sure that most men agree that if our wives/girlfriends/partners/soulmates are not happy, whole, and in balance, there is hell to pay in the relationship; there is simply no escaping it. This being the case in many situations that I have encountered, it became apparent to me that many of the men I have coached, as well as the many with whom I have had countless conversations with during my travels, were getting what I term as the "beat down" on a regular basis. Not necessarily physically, although that happens as well (we will discuss this later), but through mental and emotional altercations that were wearing them down slowly over time. Most of men's challenges were not the arguments and conflicts, nor financial issues, but rather the frustration in not knowing what to do to please their women. Sure the consistent critical comments, cynical behavior, lack of respect, and their wife's passive-aggressive actions were tough to deal with, but more importantly it was the state of her consciousness to behave in that manner that was more bothersome, and on top of that is *our* understanding and knowing that *we* as men are contributors to her state of consciousness. So one might ask, "What is the problem here? How do I restore order and be a leader in the house and in the relationship and gain the respect that I want?"

I have found that there are men who are totally unaware and even men who will not admit that they are getting the beat down—when in fact they are. I have seen the signs and also experienced some of them, which manifested in many ways, e.g. advanced aging, retreating into TV or sports or remote areas of the house, alcohol abuse, taking things out on peers and subordinates at work, seeking comfort in other women, letting the house go, not spending time with the kids…and the list goes on and on. Most men will make sincere efforts to fix things as best they can. Believe me, it is not for the lack of men trying to make things right that things still go wrong. It is in our nature to want to set things right—that is according to our definition, of course. So what *is* the problem? The problem is a lack of the understanding and recognition of our innate masculine and feminine natures as men and women. Yes, we have free choice, but how can we choose to do the right thing if we do not know all of our choices or at least have a thorough understanding of the landscape? We cannot. We just take the situation as it is dealt and hope we can hang in there long enough until things somehow change for the better.

Now, I am not saying that women are purposefully putting men through these mental and emotional challenges, although some of them certainly are, but the fact is women are carrying heavy burdens in attempting to resolve their feelings and emotions in a male-oriented society, as well as harboring the pain of traumatic experiences throughout their lives. As men it is our responsibility to help women heal from these experiences just like it is their responsibility, in turn, to heal us. Another issue is that the magnitude and potential of a woman's power and influence is not yet fully understood by men, so instead of us helping women to focus their creative energy on something beneficial to the relationship, it's redirected to all other aspects of their lives resulting in negative outcomes. It is analogous to having a nuclear generator in your house that has enough energy to keep the lights running for half your town, but you are only using it to power your toaster not realizing that all its "unapplied" energy will powerfully affect your environment one way or another.

Relationships have proven to be a major challenge for most people I know, including myself. Although I have coached numerous people on how to navigate through their relationship troubles, personally speaking, my experiences have never given me a free pass in life or a magic pill to avoid all the common issues that may arise when two people come together to be in a relationship. It really boils down to our overall perspective on life, which dictates the decisions that we make on a daily basis. What drives our decision-making process? Our decision-making is determined by our personal values in conjunction with how we perceive ourselves and our environment. That is the point of this book—to hopefully give you a broader perspective on life, love, and relationships.

Chapter 1:
My Wife Pees Standing Up

"Everything proceeds as if of its own accord, and this can all too easily tempt us to relax and let things take their course without troubling over details. Such indifference is the root of all evil."
— I Ching

Individuals and couples can have a happy and healthy relationship regardless of the challenges they may have faced in the past. Even if you acted totally and completely out of character (I mean cutting the complete fool), there is no need to hide in shame or retreat from your family—at least not if you want to make things better and are open to growth and evolution.

When I am talking to couples I always say that if Kenya and I made it, then you can too. We have been through a gamut of life challenges, e.g. our house burning to the ground, cancer, financially failed businesses, public assistance, living in group homes, domestic violence, extended family drama, police calls, and the list goes on... We share our stories because we believe they can be helpful and give others the perspective that challenges are a part of the growth process and that, unfortunately, relational dysfunction, including mistakes and bad judgments, also goes along with it, which in many cases can hurt the very ones you claim to love the most.

One thing I can say about Kenya and me is that when we have major disagreements—even in the midst of a heated conflict—we understand that in some way we are *both* contributors to the problem. We have gotten past the belief that one person is bringing the issue to the other. I have a general rule which is, that **any success or failure in a relationship is a 50/50 thing**. In other words, if the relationship is going smoothly and all parties are getting along, it is because all parties have done equal work to make it so. If things are not going well and there are fights and conflicts, then both parties are contributing equally to that situation as well. This fact may be tough for men to accept for several reasons:

13

- We have been taught to play the victim role and put the blame for our problems on everyone and everything else except for ourselves
- Most of us have been trained to look at the world through our eyes and our eyes only
- We do not understand that everything and everyone around us and in the world is a reflection of us
- We do not understand our *true* selves as men and women enough to be in touch with our innate behavior and thought patterns
- We are generally unhappy and unfulfilled and, thus, not looking so much toward conflict resolution, but toward making ourselves look and feel good.

These factors have played out in my relationship with Kenya over and over again. But although we have been in a number of arguments and fights, and the thought may have arisen, we never truly considered splitting apart as an option. This way of thinking within itself is a success from the standpoint that we still have so much to learn about ourselves through our relationship, and splitting prematurely would have inhibited our individual growth and personal evolution as people.

We met on a blind date. When I look back at the trials we have had as a couple the fact that we met on a blind date should have been the first clue that the myriad of challenges weren't something we could have ever predicted. We attracted each other based on where we were vibrationally; meaning we were both ready to learn some major lessons about ourselves and take the next step towards our individual growth. Essentially, we were both ready to get married and both interested in growing ourselves spiritually. Right away we had a lot of things in common, but at the same time we were two very different people. My realization of our differences was slow and did not come to the forefront until we were well into our marriage—children and all. Looking back, I now realize that my first "conscious" clue should have been when I used to visit her in her apartment on Sixteenth Street in Washington, DC.

We were both attending school at Howard University; I was in graduate school getting my MBA and she was an undergrad majoring in education and African American studies. Every time I was in her apartment I would hear *this noise*, and for the longest time I could not figure out what it was; it was just so strange to me. Finally, one day I heard it and decided to go investigate. The sound was coming from the bathroom. As I turned the corner and peered in, there was Kenya, PEEING STANDING UP! She just smiled at me, finished her business and walked back into the bedroom. Now, that may have been a standard for women or anyone who has been exposed to that type of thing growing up, but for me it was a complete mind blower. I asked her, "Why do you stand up and pee like that?" Her response was a big smile and a giggle and didn't resonate with me at all; I still did not understand. Now, I have definitely heard of women standing up to use the bathroom when the facilities were not clean or out in nature, but it boggled my mind why she would do that in her own apartment, which she always kept spotless. I remember telling her that I was going to write a book about it and name it "My Wife Pees Standing Up." She just laughed. That moment for me should have been the clue to all of the trials yet to come that we would face as a young couple, but at the time I did not have the insights to make any sense of it; I could only sit in bewilderment and amazement.

Why was that event relevant? Well, as I see and realize it now, the crux of our issues as a couple began in that moment with my inability to step up as a *true* man in our relationship and for her to step into her power as a *true* woman. The bottom line is my wife was looking for me to be a leader in our house and take full accountability for the state of our family, including her emotional well-being, and I was looking to her be that source of power and vision that could help us navigate through all of the challenges and unknowns we would undoubtedly face as a family. In other words, she was looking for me to operate out of my masculine nature and I was looking for her to operate out of the feminine part of hers. The symbolism of a woman peeing standing up is now clear. First of all, and most obvious, a man standing up to urinate is one of the few defining and symbolic masculine acts in the modern world for the simple fact that technology has made the accomplishment of most tasks fairly straight forward. In addition, we no longer live in the wilderness where conflicts with violent aspects of nature were once a way of life. Symbolic because it is done that way more out of preference and perhaps having a sense of power rather than out of necessity or capability. So in essence, what was being communicated is that this woman is masculine—whether she wanted to admit it or not, and whether I wanted to recognize it or not.

Second of all, if she is presumed masculine or has masculine tendencies, then it stands to reason, based on the Law of Physics and the Universe, that since two objects cannot occupy the same space at the same time and since the north side of the magnet will not attract the north side of another magnet, only the south, I must have feminine tendencies. So according to the Universal Law of Attraction her masculinity filled the masculine void that I had, and my femininity filled the feminine void that she had.

Thirdly, is the fact that these things were not recognized until later in our relationship. We had no idea what we were in for, and we definitely did not have any idea that we had major deficiencies in our masculine and feminine natures. This is a key point because people tend to get together based on what they like about each other (the positive things we recognize and that are reflected back at us) and stay away from those things that reflect the negative; consequently, there are hosts of character traits about people we just do not recognize at first glance that prove to cause major problems down the line, not because they are bad, but because those unseen character traits are reflecting something within us that we need to work through. Think about what that must say about you as a person. Let us say your wife has a major problem with lying about money, but you did not pick up on it until a year or two into the relationship, so initially this was not a problem. Upon realizing this as a problem, you could ask yourself where else do you not recognize dishonesty around money. Could it be because you have some of those tendencies as well or at least unwarranted tolerance for that behavior? Unwarranted until it really starts to impact you financially in a big way, and then you see that it *is* a problem, so you say, "I can't believe she's like that."

There was one other defining moment early on in our relationship, which would prove to be critical in our ability to live harmoniously together. We would get into the biggest arguments specifically during Kenya's menstruation cycle. I remember telling her that if we ever were to break up, it would be while she was on her period. In one sense, modern society considers these types of behaviors normal. However, from another perspective, we need to ask ourselves what is really taking place here, and not only what is taking place, but we need to question how the behavior is impacting our relationship. This is also of significance because the bottom line is that it should not be considered normal that women go through emotional turmoil during their periods. A woman's period represents a time of cleansing and renewal; replacing the old with the new, but severe pain and discomfort should be more of the exception rather than the rule. Research into how indigenous societies viewed a woman's "moon" time would reveal some further insights here.

Kenya being upset during these times was an indication not only of the overflow of masculine energy that she was carrying, but also of the pain and tension that she was storing in her reproductive organs, which actually was a sign that serious healing was necessary. When I say she stored pain in her reproductive organs I am referring to the concept of cellular memory. Everything we experience as human beings is stored as a memory in our cellular structure, but the question is which cells? Generally, for women these traumas are stored in their vagina and other reproductive organs because that is where it is most easily released from through the act of sex and their periods. Like it or not, since we attracted each other, I was charged with the task. When I said earlier that I had feminine characteristics and did not step up as a true man in our relationship, it was during these instances that I did not "show up" as I needed to. Instead of stepping in and really trying to understand what she was going through, support and comfort her during these times, and facilitate a healing process that would bring her balance, I would try to avoid her. As a matter of fact, I considered it a break time for me because I could justify not spending intimate time with her because no sex was taking place; therefore, none of the preliminary holding, caressing, and touching was needed either. It also gave me a break from sex, which, to be honest, had become a chore for me. After a while, sex in our relationship (as in many of my others) had grown to be more of an obligation rather than fun and enjoyable like it was during the first part of the relationship. I didn't understand the complete dynamics of why I felt that way at the time, but this was yet another clue that there was a major emotional healing required for her and a major educational process on gender roles for myself. That is why I have dedicated an entire chapter to healing our relationships and women through sexual and intimate interactions.

The bottom line is that I did not want to deal with the yelling, attitudes, faces, and overall emotionality; it was simply too much for me to be around. Additionally, I did not trust myself around her in those situations because things would be so unpredictable. If I was having a bad day at the same time, we would *really* be in trouble.

We need to focus on challenging issues like this in relationships if we are to continue to grow into healthy men. These types of situations should be motivating factors for us and provide us with a chance to stake our claim in the world by rebalancing and fixing a situation that desperately needs attention. And I am in no way saying that I would have to be the one to directly apply all the emotional healing myself or address the situation alone, but I definitely would be the catalyst to correct it. That is the charge of a man; it starts with himself and then his wife and family. Without applying that healing to a woman you can forget coming into manhood. As a matter of fact, I am putting forth a law or requirement for manhood, which is **a boy cannot become a man until he has healed a woman**.

One of my spiritual teachers used to define a man as "one who sets things right in the eyes of God." That statement always stuck with me because it implied so much;

especially, when we look at the world today and see how much needs to be "set right." What is implied in that definition of manhood is that a man who is fully engaging his masculine energy proactively looks for those things that need correcting and sets out to correct them. This zealousness and proactive nature is one of the key attributes of manhood that I explain later in the book. It also implies that in order for a man to set things right, he must have a proclivity towards challenges and obstacles; something about the opportunity to overcome an obstacle would have to be a naturally motivating behavioral pattern within him. There is truth about men wanting to win. Each time a man overcomes an obstacle or challenge his confidence grows. It's just like conquering levels on a video game; the higher you go, the stronger you get. Regardless of our religious or spiritual backgrounds, we as men, see things everyday that we know could be made better and that we, in one form or another, have the power to start correcting. But corrections should start at home by working on yourself first; otherwise, you bring less than your full potential to any given situation.

Another perplexing part of relating to women is dealing with women who are not only masculine in their functioning, but are also physically violent. The violence does not necessarily have to be directed at a single person, although it often is. They are just violent in general. How do you deal with someone like that? Better yet, why are they like that? The mere fact that a woman would try to exert her influence over a man or anyone else through physical means has always been puzzling to me. The challenging part is how to practically deal with these women. Most of the experiences I have had with women have shown them to be more strategic and cerebral in acquiring what they want rather than attempting to physically plow through anyone who steps in their path; however, I have seen many examples of the latter.

Relative to the universal laws, *Tame Your Woman* is also based upon the Universal Law of Creation, which states: Whatever thoughts you focus on become your beliefs. Your beliefs become your knowingness. Your knowingness influences your attitude and actions thus affecting the events that manifest in your life. Basically, the laws are universal because they can be applied to anything and everything. In this book I apply them to our masculine and feminine natures and describe how they are to interact with one another to facilitate a healthy relationship.

Chapter 2:
Tame Your Woman

– tame.
"1b : to subject to cultivation."
"3 : to tone down : soften"
(2010). Merriam-Webster Online Dictionary.

Karaba: I don't want to marry anyone. Witch or not, I will never be somebody's servant.
Kirikou: If you were my wife, you would never be my servant.
Karaba: That's what all men say before marriage.
Kirikou: I'm not like all men.
Karaba: That's true, little Kirikou. One day, you'll say all of that to a nice little girl.
Kirikou: I don't like little girls.
– from the movie Kirikou and the Sorceress by Michael Ocelot

This book is the complement to my wife's book, *Change Your Man,* which details how women can subtly change their men by first changing themselves as a result of stepping back into and using their true feminine natures. *Tame Your Woman* works the same way by having men step into their masculine natures by taming their inner woman as a method to improve their relationships.

It's time that as men we become very clear on what we want to achieve in our relationships and very intentional and overt with our actions. A statement as simple as "Yes dear, I am here and willing to help you come into your fullness as a woman" lets you know the source of the problem men have in their relationships. It is not that women do not listen and do not respect men; it's that we have not displayed the right consistent actions to earn their respect. We have not declared our intent to be there to support them emotionally, physically, or spiritually, and subsequently follow through on that declaration. We have not prioritized healing them from their childhood traumas and toxic relationships with our male counterparts. Any woman born and raised in modern cultures and who has dated or been in relationships has experienced trauma of some sort and needs some kind of healing. Yes, this is our charge as men. I know it may sound like a lot of responsibility, but it is all worth it because remember, you cannot become a man until you have tamed your inner woman and subsequently healed a woman. Anyone who thinks otherwise does not understand the universal laws governing our very existence, namely the Universal Law of Duality which says that everything has a corresponding complement and that to fulfill our destinies we must learn to work with and relate to others. For example, the only way the sperm can fulfill its destiny is to play its exact role with the egg; otherwise, forget it—everyone loses. Yes, the sperm is a complete entity in an of itself, but it is has a role outside of itself.

Men and women, when in their masculine and feminine roles, are compliments to one another and therefore cannot live to their fullest potential without mastering a healthy interaction. As a matter of fact, the entire foundation of this book is based upon the Principles of Universal Law (e.g. physics and metaphysics of time and space, complementary and supplemental relationships, etc.). The reason being is to remove the personal and emotional nonsense out of the relationship discussion and look at the fundamental aspects of our masculine and feminine nature and potential. To have a clue on how to function with others, we must first know who we are and understand our dominant tendencies as men and women. Once we can come to terms with what we need individually to fulfill ourselves, then we will understand how others can fit into our personal paradigms.

In my wife's book *Change Your Man*, the responsibility is on women to make personal changes to themselves first; thus initiating the change in their men. When these physical, mental, and emotional transformations occur, women appear and act differently, which in turn, causes the men in their lives to treat them accordingly. The same concept holds true for *Tame Your Woman*. Men need to tame their *own* nature and vices FIRST and bring forth their highest masculine talents in order to affect positive healing for the women in their lives. More specifically, men need to *tame their inner woman* so that their masculine nature can come to the forefront of their relationships, which ultimately explains this book title's dual concept of men *first* "taming their inner woman" to then tame their woman. In other words, if you want her to respect you as a man then act like one and she will without question.

Tame Your Woman is all about changing men's perspectives and habits in relationships. There is no work required by women in this book, as it is not intended for women. Men who implement the principles presented in this book will see that the women in their lives change drastically—they begin to feel more secure, appreciated, and loved, and as a result will respect you as the man you have become.

Oftentimes men respond in a feminine way to challenges in their relationships, which creates more problems in the long run. This is a result of men not having been initiated properly into manhood, but is also a result of men's unresolved issues with their mothers. Most men subconsciously blame their mothers for issues between their parents, including divorce, domestic violence, and arguments. I say "subconsciously" because if you ask most men who is to blame for the challenges in their parents' relationship or their father choosing to leave the family, they will say it is all on the father. That is our conscious perspective and the one that is most popular in modern cultures. However, this is not the whole truth and subconsciously we know it. We watched him walk out the door, so of course we think that is all there is to it. We think he is just trifling and not interested in being around his family, right? I mentioned earlier that all men have a propensity to do the right thing and I am sticking by that. The bottom line is, if a man chooses not to be at home either physically or mentally, there must be a deeper reason beyond the popular "he is not interested or is a bad father." Those explanations are part of an older paradigm that supports women being a victim and lacking equal power and equal accountability in relationships. I go more into detail on this in the *Momma* chapter.

The point of this work is not to tell anyone how they must relate or with whom they must relate too; I truly have no interest in personal preferences. All of my works are based upon one thing—empowering individuals by expanding their perception and awareness; therefore, allowing them to make more informed choices. Being informed makes all of the difference. Because my wife and I had early training in universal laws and relationships, it allowed us to know who we really were, even during arguments and conflict. I could be in the heat of a battle with her, but still have the ability to stand outside of myself and observe how absolutely foolish I was behaving. My having this ability is probably the primary reason we were able to stay together all of these years. We knew these confrontations were not us at our best, but represented an ignorance of what to do and how to function in those moments. If, in instances like that, we could just imagine that every time we "cut the fool," we could also admit to ourselves that "this is an aspect of me that does not know any better in this particular situation" —it would at least prevent us from placing the blame solely on our partners and give us room for growth.

Chapter 3:
Coming Into My Own

"My dad said, 'Boy don't you eat no pussy.' I couldn't wait to eat the pussy; he was wrong about everything else." – Richard Pryor

Throughout my many relationships, I found myself in competition with other men. I always needed to know how I compared to the other men in their past and present; a number of male friends and associates of mine felt the same way. It was critical that I was seen as special, unique, and really the ultimate guy in the eyes of whatever woman I was with. Even men who have openly denied this still behaved in such a way that showed being the ultimate man with their wife or girlfriend was of utmost importance to them. This is a key sign of the mental fragility of men when it comes to relationships.

When I was growing up no one taught me anything about sex. No one taught me about oral sex, how to penetrate and please a woman, or what women liked or did not like. The first time I had sex, I really had no idea what an orgasm was until I had one before I even entered the woman; I still put the condom on and proceeded to lose my virginity though. When you are seventeen, you can have something like twenty ejaculations and still be hard as diamonds. Those were the good old days. Today I have to do breathing exercises, visualizations, pop vitamins, and watch my diet to ensure peek performance, but that is a whole other story.

Whew, what a relief that was! Now I could talk with the fellas without faking that I had sex before. I can't begin to tell you how much of a burden it was for me to listen to other teenage boys talking about their sexual experiences and the number of girls they had been intimate with, knowing I had not been with any, and you could tell who was telling the truth and who was not—just something about the way the guys told their stories. You knew it was the kind of stuff you could not get from a magazine. We could tell when my man Darnell was telling the truth, and when Andrew was not. Darnell would act out the whole thing, and then imitate how mad his girlfriend was because he ejaculated all over her couch and Andrew would stutter his way through telling his stories. I for one would be thinking, "This dude is making this stuff up," but I understood his plight and felt his pain. Well, "What about you Carl? When was the last time you bunned a honey?" My response went something like this (remember this was in my early teens):

Me: "You know holmes, I was just killing some pussy the other night. Girl was like loving it and shit. She eventually just told me to stop because it was too much for her."

Darnell: "Whoa! That's what's up. Who was this sister?"

Me: "I can't go into all of that. Next thing I know you'll be trying to talk to her."

Darnell: "Whatever. No one's thinking about any of your ugly ass girls. Now who was it? Unless you're bullshitting like Andrew over here."

Me: "Na. Plus, you don't know her anyway. She's from Delaware and only comes up every once and a while."

But it was more like she was from La La Land because she just did not exist. I did not even have a made up mental picture of this woman. Really, I just wanted the focus of the conversation to shift to someone else. Darnell knew he was the only one getting any pussy on a regular basis anyway, but he loved to torture the rest of the guys.

Another guy who we knew was telling the truth was Brian. Brian was a tall, well-built African-American kid

29

who also attended the all-white middle school where we all went. We were the only two African-American males in the whole school. He was pretty much screwing all the girls who were willing to screw at that time. He and some of the other athletic dudes were virtually running through the whole school. You can just tell when guys are handling their business in that area because they appear to be super confidant and walk like movie stars down the school hallways. Brian would always tell us self-gratifying, big-dick jokes with a straight face because it was, at least partly, not a joke. His conversation would be like this:

Brian: "Hey Carl! Yo man, my dick is so big I can fuck myself in the ass."

Me: "Good deal Brian. That's great to hear. I was worried for a minute that you may fall short."

Brian: "Carl you getting any pussy yet? I know you like Tasha. She's fine as a motherfucker. You know I'm fucking her, right? Carl, my dick is so big that if I'm not careful when I'm screwing, it will pop through a girl's chest like in the movie Alien^{TM}. You saw that movie, right?"

Me: "That's great. Glad to know you're screwing all the girls I like."

Brian: "Yeah, when I'm getting out the shower I have to be careful not to trip over my joint. You know what I mean?"

Me: "Wow man. Glad to know you got one of the biggest dicks in the school. Hopefully, you don't trip yourself up coming out of the shower and bump your head and go into like a coma for life. I hope that doesn't happen. If that happened then I might have to holler at Tasha."

Brian: "Carl's the funny man. Holler at me when you even get in the same room as some pussy holmes so I can upgrade your 'No Pussy' card to an 'Almost Gets It' card."

The second time I had sex was with a different girl, who was my girlfriend at the time. She was from Barbados, three years my senior and was the most beautiful girl I had seen in my life. Her skin and eyes were exotic—simply beautiful—and she talked with a slight island accent. Nice!

As one would have it, eventually we had sex for the first time, which I kind of considered as my first time, because it was unprotected and I did not have an ejaculation before entering her. This experience was so different from any other that I honestly did not know what it was; while ejaculating I just stayed inside of her trying to figure out what was happening. Then as I was pulling out, I figured out what it was—the feeling of ejaculating inside of a woman with no protection was way better than ejaculating outside of her, into a condom (a bag), or through masturbation.

I mean I had seen ejaculation in pornographic movies, but it really did not register with me what was actually going on there. Besides, in pornographic movies the man never ejaculates inside the woman; it is always outside. When I had this ejaculation experience inside of my girlfriend during sex I was in complete awe—it was an interesting feeling that paralyzed me for a minute. So I withdrew my penis to see what was going on and low and behold, I had ejaculated. This was a huge experience for me because it's where I learned about ejaculation during sex first

31

hand. Until that experience I was clueless as to how it felt or what even caused it to happen in the first place. She didn't have an orgasm during this experience, but to be honest I had no idea what a woman's orgasm even was.

The other good thing about my experience with my girlfriend was that she taught me how to kiss. I can still remember how we kissed to this day because it was the slowest and most sensual thing I had ever experienced to that point, and on top of all of that, it felt great. All of my life I have had women tell me I was a great kisser and it's really all because of her. This experience was of major importance to me because it did two things: (1) it taught me that women like when you take your time with them and (2) it taught me that what I had seen on television around sex to that point was mostly bullshit. The kissing and sex on television was usually fast and sloppy and lacked any real sensuality, intensity, or true feeling. So for the first time I began to question television as an authority for what love and sex was all about. Don't get me wrong, I still watched the porno and R rated movies whenever I could, but at least I had a new point of reference.

My whole point in sharing my boyhood experiences with sex and relating to women is that I really had no training about what it means to please a woman, let alone how to treat her. As a young man my experiences were all driven by peer pressure for the most part and my education was through television and the stories my friends told. But the impact goes beyond sex. It also impacted how I viewed and treated women. Because I didn't have an understanding of a woman's nature—what made them unique and different from men, or why I should love them, I couldn't deliver when it came to relationships.

I remember with that same girlfriend from Barbados when her birthday came around and I didn't buy her anything. If she was upset she never showed it, but all of her friends and mine teased me and laughed incessantly during school that day. I had to scramble to get her something to bring to her house later that day and still ended up loosing the gift before getting there. There were two major important lessons in that experience: (1) you need to show your wife or girlfriend public displays of love and (2) birthdays and holidays matter. I'm still learning these lessons to be honest, but the reason why I had such a challenge doing the right things around these special days was because I couldn't understand why a woman would prioritize these times of the year. For me it didn't matter either way, but the point is women and men are different in more ways than I was ever taught or cared to acknowledge; and to think, just seven years later I would be engaged.

Chapter 4:
A Look at Relationships

"Sometimes you have to forego doing what's popular in order to do what's right." – Mo'Nique

One of the questions we have to answer is, "Why do we get into relationships?" What is the point? I really do not think most people spend enough time asking themselves this question and subsequently searching for the true answer. I say that because answering this question inevitably leads us to a journey of understanding our true selves. Who am I? What am I here to do and how do I accomplish it? What are my passions in life? What brings me joy and happiness? If money was not an issue, how would I spend my time? These questions are important because on some level your life partner needs to reflect and support your path to fulfillment. From another perspective, it would be good to ask these questions and have an idea of who you are and where you want to go for the sake of any person you bring into your life. There is no need to waste anyone else's time by telling them one thing, only to end up doing another once you realize your true passions; it is particularly unfortunate if you have allowed them to invest time and energy into goals consisting of kids, career, and retirement, only for you to find out you want much more or something different.

In a discussion with my wife one night, I realized one of the more popular reasons for why we form relationships—people look to someone else to justify their value, which in turn, leads to their happiness and fulfillment. Think about that before you agree or disagree. Everyone wants to be happy and feel good about life, but what is our methodology for getting us there? Generally, we can find the people we like, consistently engage those individuals, and find a sense of joy from the interactions. But why does one person versus another make us happy, or what qualifies someone as a friend? Oftentimes it is someone with whom we feel good about being around because we share common interests, we are comfortable with them, or in some way they acknowledge our existence. This person does not have to be someone who agrees with you all the time because one of the greatest ways to know you are alive is to meet some resistance—bumping your opinions and beliefs against someone else's can be an invigorating experience, especially with a friend.

As people change or as we discover the real character of the people we are with, a natural reflex is to attempt to contain that change in behavior, especially when that behavior is something that no longer justifies our existence. For example, if you have a personal belief that your self-worth or value is primarily measured by being the only man your wife finds attractive or can be in love with, any actions contradicting that belief will be met with serious resistance, and in most cases cause either a direct confrontation or, at the very least, cause self-doubt, depression, or stress.

Some common relationship myths and false beliefs are:

1. My wife can and should love only me
2. Marriage is for people who are in love
3. I can only be happy with this person
4. My wife is responsible for my happiness
5. I have the right to have sex with my wife whenever I choose

These are but a few of the common relationship beliefs that, if contradicted, could destabilize an otherwise strong union. If the foundation of a man and woman coming together is because a person justifies (or helps to justify) our very existence, we have put ourselves at risk from the outset. The same holds true for our happiness. If we rely on others to make use happy, we are ultimately setting ourselves up for failure.

Before we dismiss the notion that we find happiness and fulfillment in others, we need to seriously examine our behavior in relationships—not only the success to failure ratio, but also the way we actually function. If this person is not the complete center of your existence, what is the issue? Why the anger, depression, and sadness? Why during arguments do we act like it is a life or death event—do or die? It would be worth taking some time to analyze our functioning in relationships, as well as the justifications we give ourselves for acting the way we do.

Chapter 5:
The World is Our Reflection

"No one has ever done anything to me. I create my life. I take 100% responsibility for all the causes of my effects... I am both."
– Kenya K. Stevens

Everything and everyone around us is simply a reflection of us according to the universal law of oneness. The universal law of oneness states that we each are at the center of the universe and that everything around is a manifestation/reflection of our thoughts and energy. This is an important principle that we must grasp to get the most out of our relationships and our entire lives. It is also a concept that greatly assists us in taking responsibility for our behavior and experiences regardless of whether we consider them triumphs or failures. One of the major challenges in relationships is that we tend to blame others for doing something to cause our unhappiness; thus justifying us to act in a particular way. It's important for us as men to see how our behavior has contributed to our relationship environment. I hear a lot men describe their wives as emotional, childish, disrespectful, etc., but fail to see any of these same qualities in themselves. It's funny how we think we are mature, confident, darn near flawless individuals who somehow attracted this childish person into our life, not realizing that metaphysical law says that you and your partner bring about the same *positives* and *negatives* to the relationship. I know, her negatives far outweigh yours and yours don't really impact the relationship like that. Your friends or coworkers maybe, but not her.

You might ask, "How can I make that assertion? What or where is the proof?" Well, the only way you can really prove this principle is to take the time to observe yourself and the people around you. In fact, the only way to truly understand anything in life is to experience it first hand so you can take ownership of it. But before that can happen, we first must comprehend the meaning of the word "understand." To understand implies to submit yourself to a situation so that you can experience it fully. For example, when our loved ones are opening their hearts to

39

us and asking if we understand them, they are really asking, "Did you transcend your preconceived thoughts of me, our situation together, and all the things you think you know about me enough to really feel where I am coming from and how I am perceiving this specific situation—or did you stay completely within your ego, which is hard and unbending and not allow yourself the opportunity to experience something new, namely me?" The real question here is, "Did you experience me *in that moment?*" If your answer is no, then you cannot make any progress toward improving your relationships because you are still using the same intellect and old patterns that were instrumental in creating the conflicts and problematic situations you are presently experiencing. Why? Because there is no *understanding*; therefore, there is a low probability of you perceiving the situation correctly and subsequently making the right choices.

So essentially, once we profess to understand our wives and how they feel and are viewing things, it allows us an opportunity to determine whether we may be feeling the same way as she or if we are doing things in a similar manner. In other words, what is she reflecting in me? Is she reflecting a part of me that I do not like: someone who is over emotional, regardless of how it is expressed, or who likes to engage in conflict? But I will save the relationship protocols until later in the book and attempt to lay some groundwork that will guide you through the exercise of understanding that our mates reflect us—they are us and we are them.

Self Perception

Can we assume that we all have talents and strengths, but also have areas within our character and personality that need improvement? Can we assume that we may know many of our talents and strengths, but not all, and that the same holds true for our weaknesses? Can we also assume that there is a part of us (this actually is a very large part of us) that we know absolutely nothing about, which is okay because we have not been put into the life situations that will allow or force those traits to come to the fore? In totality we are complete beings made up of the things we like about ourselves, the things we do not like or would like to improve upon, and some things we know nothing about. So we have established how we view ourselves and that our view or perception is based on our overall awareness. The following graphic is an attempt to illustrate three parts of our awareness. Remember, this graphic depicts simply what we think of ourselves and not who and what we are.

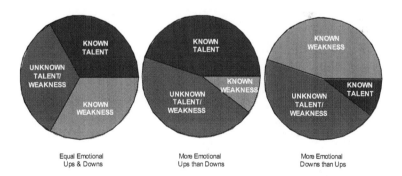

Equal Emotional Ups & Downs   More Emotional Ups than Downs   More Emotional Downs than Ups

I wanted to highlight these three aspects of knowing oneself– the talents we are aware of and like, our known weaknesses that we dislike, and the unknown aspects of ourselves; because when conflicts arise we are often quick to deny our contribution to the situation as if we have a complete understanding of ourselves and our partners. What's even more interesting is how we don't take full responsibility during these situations even when they are the same or similar to other situations we have found ourselves in. Are you really sure you aren't part of the problem here? Are you sure she is just acting crazy as hell?

Emotional State

The above diagram illustrates how we view ourselves, but in any given state, how do we actually feel emotionally? Because it is how we view a situation that governs how we feel about it. If our perception is that someone else has violated us, we tend to feel angry, vengeful, or abused. When we perceive that others have been taken advantage of, we may feel sad, remorseful, hurt, or a sense of helplessness. Generally, when we are operating within our strength or comfort zone, we feel good and in control because our confidence is high so we move toward that situation without hesitation. You could say we are vibrating at a high energy level and our blood is really flowing. An example of this would be a job interview in which your prospective employer has indicated you have performed extremely well in your previous two interviews and expects you will do the same in the last interview as well. So if someone were to ask you about your chances to get the job, you may respond, "I feel good about it." Why? It's because your perception is that the company is looking favorably at you and that your interviewing skills are more than adequate to secure the position, and basically, it is a lock.

That positive outlook translates into a positive feeling; therefore, the first piece of our formula is that perception directly impacts feeling, which is illustrated in the following diagram:

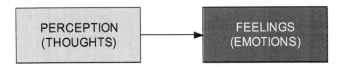

PERCEPTION (THOUGHTS) ⟶ FEELINGS (EMOTIONS)

So from the above example, we have the following:

PERCEPTION = The company likes me; the job should be a lock.
FEELINGS = I feel confident and overall really good about life right about now.

The flipside of this is when we operate within our weaknesses or when we are in areas we are not familiar with and do not feel comfortable in, we tend to feel insecure or badly, and in these scenarios we experience stress and tension. Expanding your awareness of the relationship between perception and feelings will give an understanding of the full impact of how our thoughts shape our reality.

Earlier I stated that our perceptions of the reality around us shapes our thoughts, and as a result, influences our feelings, which is another way of saying feelings are emotions. Our emotions, in turn, dictate our energetic pattern or vibration. This is significant because it is our vibration that controls what we attract into our lives. Emotions and vibrations actually are the same; however, emotions are short-term expressions of vibration, whereas your overall vibration is essentially the summation of your emotions over time. A similar relationship holds true for vibrations and our actual physiology, wherein the longer we are in a vibration pattern, the more it shapes and affects our physical form and the physical reality around us. We see this occurring with diseases like cancer in which our negative feelings around ourselves manifest as the ultimate elimination of the corresponding organ. For example, metaphysically, negative feelings around our sexuality can result in debilitation of the organs and glands that promote its healthy expression (e.g. prostate, uterus, breasts, or other reproductive organs).

The diagram below completes the model for all modalities discussed thus far.

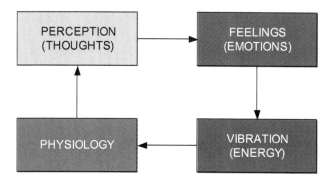

The last important note here is that our physiology or physical makeup has a direct impact on our thoughts. An example of this would be if I am a professional athlete in peak condition and working out regularly, my thought patterns will be completely different from someone fifty pounds overweight, who does not exercise and eats fast food and cakes all day. What one person views as a challenge, the other may view as an opportunity and so on.

The point of this chapter is to provide insights on what makes us tick, as well as insights on how to shift the emotions and physiology of ourselves and of the people who are directly in our lives. As men, the key is to be consistent in actions that positively impact the thoughts and beliefs about ourselves, our loved ones, as well as their general outlook on the relationship and on life, for that matter. We must continually establish and shape the foundations in our relationships so that the psyche of those we are accountable for remains optimistic and intact.

The other point is that we need to look more deeply into how we are functioning in relationships before making a conclusion, especially if we don't want to use the blame or victimization tag. There is a lot we don't know about ourselves and even more we don't know about our partners that, in all likelihood, have contributed greatly to some of the relationship woes you have experienced in your life.

Chapter 6:
Innate Masculine Traits of Man

"Initiate yourself through life or by initiated by it; it's your choice." – Rakhem Seku

The following chapters explain the inherent masculine makeup of a man, the unique masculine talents at his disposal, and how he views the world. It is important to understand these characteristics and talents have a major impact on women on both a conscious and subconscious level; thus men and women not acknowledging they exist can cause issues in our relationships.

It is also important to note that all men have some of these masculine talents or components already activated; some more strongly than others. We all come into the world with natural abilities, but we also come into the world with character deficiencies to work on. To maximize any part of our masculine potential, we must first nurture those naturally occurring masculine talents within us, but also receive formal training and coaching relative to their use; both the natural masculine talent and training in their application are requirements to become fully proficient in using them. For example, you may have natural leadership qualities, but will still need training on how to apply them in your specific career. A leader in the political arena functions differently than a leader in corporate America or on a sports team.

The four masculine traits are the Monk, Leader, Soldier, and Negotiator. Each of these masculine traits is explained in detail throughout the following chapters starting with the Monk.

Chapter 7:
Masculine Trait #1: The Monk

"What should you do in this situation? Well, you better do something or else you'll be sleeping in the streets." – *Professor Peabody, NCSU*

The Monk is a person who spends a significant amount of time searching for the truth of his existence and of life in general. He wants to know what should be done to achieve the ultimate goal in life, which is usually spiritual transcendence. Spiritual transcendence is described as physically living in the world but not being of it, meaning although you fully participate in and enjoy life, you are not obligated to feel, act, or respond either physically, emotionally, or mentally in any particular way or in any given circumstance. In other words, your highest self or greatest level of consciousness is beyond both time and space and transcends your temporal life on earth. We perceive that we are bound by time or space limitations when in fact we can transcend those limitations by identifying with that part of ourselves that operates based upon the oneness of all things. More on that in another work.

A Monk has two primary activities: 1) understanding the purpose of his life as well as his environment; and 2) setting a direction and set of objectives for his life and those to whom he is accountable based upon that purpose. So how does this apply to men who have chosen to take part in the larger society (who do not live on a mountain top and meditate all day), and specifically as it pertains to their relating to women? From the average man's perspective the same principles apply, as men should also spend a significant amount of time understanding their life's purpose and their environment (e.g. social, economic, etc.) so that they may know *what* should be done to advance their interests along with those of their wives, families, and communities. He shouldn't just spend time understanding his purpose, but should also spend time understanding the life purpose, aspirations, and talents of his wife and children. To know what to do in life, men must have an understanding and appreciation for their environment—in other words, wisdom. This is the very first responsibility for a man in any relationship with a woman.

In practical terms, the obtainment of wisdom should take two forms: 1) taking the time to learn and utilize specific processes to acquire wisdom through one's own efforts; and 2) seeking counsel from those who have knowledge in the various areas of life affecting you and your family (e.g., finances, health, relationships, child rearing, etc.).

To accelerate learning and to help avoid mistakes in judgment, the first form requires that we select and learn these processes from a capable teacher, and once understood they should be practiced in real-life scenarios until some level of proficiency is achieved.

The second form necessitates finding an expert in each particular area of concern to receive specialized counsel on what should be done to achieve success in the respective area; note that an expert in one area most likely would not be the expert in another and realistically, you can expect to have numerous individuals you talk to for advice on various matters. This expert counsel need not be expensive and can come in many ways, such as family, elders, or others in our lives who would gladly offer their perspective on any situation or challenge we are confronted with. But in all cases, it is up to you to make use of them and listen to their words and advice. This process in itself can be humbling, but it is the smartest way to go, especially for men in relationships.

Taking the perspective on getting advice from capable experts a step further, there are two growth aspects of getting counsel from others: 1) actually going and listening to the counsel; and 2) implementing it. Both aspects can be difficult because men do not like to admit what they do not know. As I stated earlier, our inherent nature tells us we are "knowers." Nonetheless, there is great value in doing both of these exercises. Going for counsel is all about first identifying someone you trust and respect and then making the time to do it. Following the counsel is a whole different story. Why should you follow someone else's advice, especially when they do not really know your situation on an intimate level and will not have to deal with the consequences? I know from experience this is not easy, but it is something we must consider. In all honesty, the accuracy of the advice is not the point here; it's the exercise of asking and subsequently following through with the advice that counts. This is what develops the humility needed to receive insight not only from others, but also from your own intuition. I realize there could be danger in following incorrect advice, but trust me things will work out fine in the end and you will develop stronger intuitive muscles in the process. On the flip side, there is a danger in following your own advice as well, so try to keep an open mind. Let's leave it there for now.

Once we as men determine what the focus of the family or relationship is, it becomes both the driving force and lodestar for everything going forward. This is a major responsibility, as it requires a level of detachment from our personal likes and dislikes as well as our current beliefs and understanding. In addition, we need to be in touch with our wife and children to ensure the overall family or relationship goals are in alignment with their individual personal goals.

As mentioned previously, an aspect of the Monk's personality is the desire to truly understand reality, especially the immediate environment. This is important because proper understanding increases the probability of

making correct choices in life, including setting the
proper expectations for what can be achieved.

Direction Setting

Early in our marriage, I was more inclined to set the
overall direction for the family (which at the time was just
my wife and me). But over a period of time, I gave up
some of that responsibility to my wife, which turned out
to be a major mistake. I say that not because she is
incapable of making good choices or setting goals, but
rather because she really had no desire to be in that
position in the first place. She would have preferred to
have me engaged enough in the relationship and
channeling the kind of confidence necessary to keep the
family moving forward. The temptation to ask my wife
what to do in certain situations was high because of her
intelligence and intuitive abilities, and it seemed logical
to ask her opinion on something because she was smart
and especially because she was right there. But
consulting your wife should be the exception not the rule,
at least until you have done significant research on your
own by talking to other knowledgeable people and
making the necessary inquiries before bringing questions
to her. Why? It lowers her stress level knowing you are
in control of the situation and are simply coming to her
for her input rather than as a result of you not knowing or
not trying. Also, if she senses that she is the first person
you come to for insight, it causes her to lose confidence in
you as a man, which will manifest as a lack of respect and
trust. You are the man, so go out into the world and get
the answers, and share what you have found in
combination with your analysis and opinion. Remember,
I am not saying that men are better goal and direction
setters across the board than women. What I am saying is
that metaphysically, setting a goal for the family and
subsequently taking full accountability for it is a

masculine activity and if you want to develop long term trust with your wife you need to make every effort to step into this role.

On the other hand, if you were to ask various women, they may disagree with this notion and want you to ask them for their input on a variety of matters, even up front—but do not fall for it! Do your research first and then present it once you have all your facts together. What we need to understand is that oftentimes women do not understand what makes themselves tick, which unknowingly results in them actually doing things to emasculate you without even realizing they are doing it— remember, the basic Law of Physics implies that the emasculation of you equates to the de-feminization of her. The results are tragic, and the discontent for the relationship will grow without anyone understanding why. In fact, this is what is happening to relationships all over; men are making choices to ask their wife's advice on major issues confronting the family, but this communicates the wrong messages to her subconscious mind. It shows that you don't have things under control and she must do something, else disaster awaits, or in short, this guy is incompetent. I know that may sound extreme, but it's true. The proof is that from that moment forward she will begin taking control of direction setting activities in the relationship.

Because of her inherent nature, my wife felt more comfortable with me being the one accountable and responsible for answering to and defending our family's position and direction to friends, relatives, and the outside world. This was especially true around the holidays when I would sit down man-to-man with our fathers or uncles and talk about the state of our family, which would always come up. She wanted me front and center defending the plan and explaining why we would be all right, even if we were experiencing some tough times at that moment. During these discussions I performed intellectual acrobatics, along with the exchange of ideas and philosophical views on my family, thinking that was expected, whereas, unbeknown to me, it was my level of *confidence* that was the key. After some time, I realized that on a subconscious level, they actually were asking whether I was confident in my abilities to navigate the family, or if I had thought through the details of a situation and considered all possible scenarios. For instance, in regards to the children, had I thought about how they would fare in a given situation.

What I also began to notice over time, was that as my wife began to make more choices on behalf of the family, it started to stress her out. Her assumption was that there was a void in direction setting, and naturally, she was going to fill it. Not only that, but she also started to resent me a bit and lose a certain amount of respect for me as a man. After all, if she was going to make the tough choices and be held accountable for them, then *what* was my role—obviously, not to keep her out of harms way. Remember, making a choice on behalf of others is a major power move and from one perspective requires wisdom, but also requires a level of fearlessness, as no one knows what the future holds. As the man in the family, I should have been willing to walk into the unknown first and take the initial hits that come from cutting a new path.

As a result of the lack of understanding of our true masculine and feminine roles, many of the changes that took place in my marriage were subtle and not noticeable until after some major events or disruptions had taken place. By then it was hard to change because we had both become comfortable in our positions relative to running the household, and with the status of our relationship it was not always easy to make major leadership changes.

Do you have any set goals in life? If you do, how did you determine what they are and how long it will take you to achieve them? Better yet, what is the purpose of your life, and what path must you follow to justify and honor your purpose? Okay, so you may have that one under control, but looking from a broader viewpoint, what about your purpose and life path along with those of your wife and children? Do you know and understand what they want to achieve in life based upon their passions, talents, and aspirations? How about your children? Are their talents artistic, musical, academic, or in the areas of teaching, researching, carpentry, engineering, playing football, nuclear physics, or philosophy? Do they need to be in public or private schools or maybe homeschooled? To cultivate these talents, you need to know the kinds of programs they should be in, as well as when and in which part of the world you should live in to properly integrate everyone's interests. This is important because we are all born with unique gifts and talents and the sooner they are recognized, the sooner they can be developed.

One of the more complex things for us to do is to set the direction for our entire life, because to do so requires that we know who we are in that very moment as well as who and where we will be at our final destination. This is no small task, as it requires that we really take the time to focus on ourselves—which by the way, I strongly suggest that we do. The ability to set one's direction precedes the requirement for leadership, as a leader must first receive counsel on their goals and objectives from those who are wiser. The fact is that most people do not know who they are, where they ultimately want to go, or what their true passions are in life. The primary reason for this in many cases is because we are conditioned to respect other people's opinions of us in a higher regard than our own. In many respects, we do not trust ourselves because oftentimes our desires contradict logic or social protocol and just the thought of that contradiction instills fear in our hearts.

Starting in the first grade, it is our teachers who tell us what success and failure looks like and what the important subjects are to learn. Our parents select our religion, the food we eat, who we play with and when we play, what we wear, where we live, what instruments and sports we play, and so on. This is all a good thing when we are at a young age because we are not capable of effectively communicating our desires, so having others set us on our path is important; plus the fact that our desires at a young age could get us into trouble if we are not careful. For example, our desire at age three to run into the street to get a ball does not need to be honored, nor will it get us very far in life. But as we mature as men and begin to recognize that time should be taken to understand ourselves and families more, we are empowered to make more informed decisions going forward.

A natural tendency in men is to want to set the direction for others, even above themselves. I have observed this throughout my life with my male friends and business associates. Men will "go to blows," to say the least, to have a say in how things should go, whether it is relative to business, relationships, or social issues. What I have also observed is when a man is in a situation in which he has no say, he will first remove himself mentally from that situation, and then remove himself physically. I have observed this in many churches and religious organizations. Oftentimes within these organizations there are a few men in charge of the entire operation of the organization; we will call them the Tier 1 leadership team. Below them is Tier 2 consisting of a large group of mostly women who are drawn to their power and leadership qualities, and finally, a group of men who are on the outskirts as a Tier 3 class within the organization.

The psychology of the Tier 3 male group is fascinating, as they are generally drawn to the organization because of its philosophy, but also the large number of women in the second and fourth tiers, as well as potential leadership opportunities, but because they have no real power within the organization, they generally grow frustrated and disenfranchised and eventually leave—mentally first, then physically. The Tier 3 males tend to be a revolving door of members, whereas the first and second tiers are more stable. Their frustration is because of an inability to express their core character attributes in a group setting, which in this case, would be having their ideas heard and implemented, then followed by acknowledgement. Let's be clear, in no way am I saying every man's opinion or idea should be implemented or even heard for that matter; however, it does not change the strong urge a man has to express himself in this way. Another point to note with this example is that the group setting provides and encourages even more passion to express this direction-setting energy because the acknowledgment potential is greater. Let's face it, catching the game-winning pass in a championship football game with no time left on the clock, in front of 80 thousand people live and another 20 million on television is the ultimate high. How many of us as boys dreamt of hitting the game-winning shot at the buzzer and acted it out a thousand times, including the cheers in the background, the fouls, and the interview afterwards? I know I sure did, and believe me, if the shot did not go in, then I got fouled.

Women respect and are drawn to men who know where they are going in life and show zealous movements toward that direction. I can assure you that it is not the goal itself that women are drawn to; the attractive part is men's ability to pick goals and stick with them, in addition to their ability to make the hard choices and follow through regardless of personal or social pressures.

The ultimate objective a man selects is lower in the hierarchy than demonstrating the ability to select and stick to the objective. Why? Because the reality is that things change, and the probability that you will have to alter or abandon an existing goal or create new ones based on changes in environmental or family dynamics is high, if not outright guaranteed. Not only that, but we also need to set goals almost on a daily basis. It is true some goals are long term and require less reworking, but on a micro level we have things to accomplish today, this week, this month, and so forth. Plus, as a general rule, you always want to be as close to the source of a creation as possible, as opposed to the end of creation itself. In other words, it is more important to have the skill of setting direction and choosing objectives for yourself and others than simply having a goal that you obtained from who knows where.

In my days as a technical consultant, I always wondered how I could receive credit for being a top performer if I were constantly empowering my teammates and those who I competed against for raises and promotions. During the evaluation process, we were measured on our ability for being "value creators" or one who could create valuable ideas, tools, deliverables, procedures, and artifacts no matter what project we were assigned; however, in most cases it seemed as though after I had created and completed a deliverable or artifact, I had to turn it over to my superiors or other peers and not receive direct credit for the work in most cases. After a while, I realized that the value was not in the artifact itself (the report or research I produced), but in my ability to consistently create quality solutions to common business problems. As such, I became a "value creator" within my company, rather than a holder and distributor of created value. The same could hold true with me developing people to be leaders and assets to the company; it is more valuable to take someone who lacks leadership characteristics and confidence and teach them to become leaders, even to the point where they can teach others. In doing so, I have just reduced the burden on the company from having to find leaders in the open market as well as reducing internal battles for projects to secure the most talented people from within the company.

So from one perspective, our ability to set a direction for ourselves and those we are responsible for requires wisdom and understanding. It is a serious charge and really not one for a younger person who has not experienced the world around him. It requires counsel and knowledgeable people who can help you look at all the shaping factors so that the proper direction can be set.

What if I'm Wrong
You're going to be wrong sometimes or even often; that's not even the question. Being a Monk has nothing to do with being right all the time. It has more to do with establishing an energy of interest, focus, and dedication to yourself and your family. Just the idea of you consistently thinking ahead for you and the family will help develop a stronger bond and more trust and support in your relationship.

Benefits and Affects to the Feminine Traits in Women:
Living proficiently as a Monk will assist your wife's ability to come into her Visionary personality trait; thus she will have more faith and trust in you as a man. The Visionary is a feminine part of our personality that is

most dominant in women and enables us to have faith that everything will work out for the best in the end. It's our ability to be optimistic even in the face of challenge and adversity. The faith comes from her understanding and experiencing that you are focused on the future of her and the family. It will also begin to open up her Devotee personality trait enabling her to be more receptive to you. The Devotee is also a feminine part of our personality that is most dominant in women and enables us to hold the mental image of our desire; thus, helping us stay committed to our goals.

Monk Self-Test

This test will give you an idea of your ability to be a Monk based on your actions as a man to date. The questions are straightforward and contain content you may take for granted, so I recommend that you take your time and answer honestly to ensure you capture the most accurate score for each section. These questions are for you to evaluate your proclivity as a Monk, as opposed to a game to try and get the highest score or compete with your friends.

Monk Self-Test Questions

	Question	Considerations	Score
1.	Do you set goals for yourself and your family on a cyclical basis (i.e. annual, monthly, etc.)? These goals are known and understood by your wife and children (depending on age, of course).	Yes = 1 No = 0	
2.	Do you have elders or experts in your life who	Relationships Yes = 1	

	give you advice in the key areas of finance and relationships? *Note: The only exception here is if you are an expert (based on formal experience and training only) in one of these areas, but even so, it's good to have some support.*	No = 0 Finances Yes = 1 No = 0	
3.	Do you know (or at least think you may know) your life's purpose? Your life's purpose can include one or all of the following: what your passions are around people, career, activities, etc.; how you want to contribute to the world to make it a better place, or knowing the major things you want to do and accomplish before you die.	Yes = 1 No = 0	
4.	Are you the one who generally initiates and decides what the family plans are for the day, weekend, week, or month? *Note: This is not determining how things get done; only what needs to be done. Determining how things get done is a feminine trait.*	Yes = 1 No = 0	
		Your Total	

Earned	
Total Possible	5

Monk Self Test Rating Summary

5 out of 5 – Proficient
4 out of 5 – Good
3 out of 5 – Needs Improvement
2 out of 5 – Seriously Deficient
1 or 0 out of 5 – Complete Monk Character Void

Developmental Processes: The Monk

These developmental processes are practical exercises any man can use to strengthen their own Monk masculine personality trait. The following exercises will develop the talents of intuition and humility.

Monk Developmental Process #1:

Meditation and deep contemplation are the best tools to gain insights on various life matters. If nothing else, the contemplative process opens us up to receiving information that we would normally be closed to or otherwise not recognize.

Think of a challenge that you and the family may be having and set aside some time to meditate or think in solitude about possible solutions. You should find a place that will allow you the mental space to accomplish this task, preferably away from friends and family. This time should be used only to think about solutions to the issue that you have selected. To do this effectively, you must first realize that you may not understand the issue itself, so part of this time must be used to understand what you are up against. Like they say, knowing the problem is half the solution.

Pay very close attention to the thoughts and ideas that enter your mind and DON'T DISMISS THEM. Rather, write them down if you don't understand so you can contemplate them further at another time. It's important to understand that your intuition is not logical or analytical. The thought doesn't have to make sense per se. As a matter of fact, that's how you can tell intuition from logical thinking; if the thought is something that can be easily explained or proven it's probably arrived at through reasoning. We want to learn to embrace what's extraordinary and unconventional as well was what's logical as the best solutions are often times outside of the box.

Monk Developmental Process #2:

Determine the three biggest areas of your life and find competent, experienced mentors in each area. Some examples of key life areas are social, relationship, sexual, financial, health, educational, business, spiritual, and religious. Devise a yearly plan for each of the areas and ensure you have concurrence from each of your mentors. Set up quarterly check-in points to make sure you are progressing as planned. Remember, the point here is to learn the process for gaining an understanding by literally submitting to and standing under the counsel of others. The requirement is not to follow advice blindly, but to at least listen to what is being said and strongly consider it as an option.

Make yourself available to be a mentor for someone who needs your expertise and insights. Be on the lookout for these individuals, as they may not approach you directly. Being a mentor and guide will help you appreciate how to follow the advice of others.

Chapter 8:
Masculine Trait #2: The Leader

"Knowing is not enough, you must apply; willing is not enough, you must do." – Bruce Lee

Leadership is one of the least understood character traits in modern culture. Part of the issue is an overall lack of understanding of the makeup of men's consciousness in general, but even more so around a lack of recognition of the masculine nature as a separate, distinct, and necessary quality in life. Yes, leadership is a masculine trait, and yes, men have a natural inclination and talent to lead and manage others; the opportunity to do that is critical in any man's growth and development.

I have identified six aspects of leadership that men should develop to strengthen their skills in this area. However, before we embark on the leadership journey, let's discuss as a prerequisite that any man serious about developing his leadership capabilities should consider getting on a cardiovascular regiment to increase his body's ability to process oxygen through strengthening the heart and lungs. If we presume that oxygen is the elemental power we intake that energizes and maintains the entire body, then our ability to think, heal, and handle stress correlates to our ability to optimize our utilization of oxygen.

The Problem is Choice

In the movie The Matrix Reloaded ^{TM}, the main character, Neo, discovered that the key to human survival against the machines was our ability to choose. The power of choice is the primary key to strengthening the leader within, but unfortunately, most men do not understand choice.

> ### Choice is defined as:
>
> *The ability to select the best course of action to achieve a goal or objective based on an accurate understanding of the current environmental conditions and the selected strategic plan.*

That sounds easy enough to do, but let's analyze the definition of choice to ensure we fully understand.

- "The ability to select…"

The ability to select implies that we have multiple options in most situations and that we are free to choose the best option available. This may seem obvious, but there are many cases in which we as men feel as though we do not have options when, in fact, we always do. To say we are without options is to imply that we are powerless, and to say we are powerless is to say that we are victims. We may be under attack or in a rough situation, but it is just that, a rough situation. Within these situations, we will see that we have a number of choices, and usually the choice or choices we make will determine the collateral damage sustained during the challenges.

- "…the best course of action…"

First, "action" means there is movement as a result of our selection; movement means change and that others will be affected in some way. So the bottom line is that this choice matters to someone. Second, "best" implies there is a superior action to take over all others to achieve our end goals. But how do we know what action is best? It helps if we can evaluate our options based on how they will facilitate the desired outcome without our personal bias. Looking at something without bias requires that we take all attachments and emotionality out of the decision-making process; hence, giving us a rule for being an effective leader—*Leader Rule #1: The best actions are taken in the absence of emotion.*

- "...to achieve a goal or objective..."

Of course, everything we do is about achievement and moving our lives forward, but do we have clear goals for our future? Goals in our lives represent lodestars that we follow to a specific destination. These goals are never the end all because it is human nature to always desire more. Plus, life does not end just because we have success. In relationships we should have goals for ourselves, wives and children, extended families, and communities. Set by the Monk part of our personalities, goals are our foundation for the decisions we make and the actions we take in our lives, as discussed in the chapter on the Monk.

This statement also ties together the Leader and Monk personality traits and shows how they relate to one another. The Monk sets the goals and the Leader implements and takes one hundred percent accountability for them.

- "...based on an accurate understanding of the current environmental conditions..."

A leader is always aware of current conditions (economic, social, physical, etc.) around him. This includes the physical and mental state of those he is and is not responsible for, as well as anything in the environment that may directly or indirectly affect his family. The key here is awareness or presence of mind, which translates into really noticing and looking closely at all the intricacies and subtleties of the physical phenomena around us. What's important here is that we are talking about actual *current* conditions as opposed to what could be. As a Leader you have to call it like you see it. It's said that you need to know where you are at to know where you are going, right?

When we hear metaphysical teachers discussing living in the present, they are usually talking about the leadership trait, which incidentally, is one of nine possible states of awareness. In other words, we can choose to be here in the present and accept things as they are or we can choose to project our desired reality by creating a mental image of where we want to be. The leadership faculty requires that we be present with all that is around us and experience it for what it is; to take it all in so to speak. This is one aspect of being in the present, but in truth we must live in the physical and mental realms equally; thus, we are not always focused on just our physical surroundings.

- "…and the selected strategic plan."

A goal represents what you want to achieve in life, whereas the plan represents *how* you will achieve it. For every goal there must be a plan. The plan defines what is required to achieve the goal and the specific steps to get us there. A plan is not developed by the leader, but rather by a strategist or someone who understands how things get done and in what order. A true strategist, which by the way is a feminine trait, must live in both the physical and mental realms because developing a strategy requires insight into the unseen. It requires assumptions, vision, and faith in the creative laws responsible for bringing things into fruition. That is very important because many leaders make the mistake of thinking they have the inherent skills to define both what should be done and how it should be done when in fact a leader better defines who should do it to achieve the maximum result. I will repeat this a few times throughout the book because men need to honor the balance of power with their wives; else, failure will be the result. It is the strategists or visionaries (feminine trait), not leaders that come up with the plan for getting things done; thus in relationships, we can say women are responsible for saying how the plans are implemented.

A leader, on the other hand, defines who does the tasks and ensures the resources are there to get them done. Loosely translated, a man in his full masculine leadership personality needs guidance from others on a strategy of action. This holds true in leading the family as well. A man who is in control of resources and is responsible for ensuring things get done correctly should not assume he knows how to get them done. As stated before, the creation of the strategy is actually a feminine attribute and responsibility in a relationship. The man in his full masculine nature can say *what* (the Monk) he wants to achieve, but a woman in her full feminine nature is best suited to tell you *how* (the Visionary) to achieve it. This is the balance of power in relationships that is set up by nature. So if you are in the position of giving direction and also dictating how things are accomplished, you have an imbalance in the relationship from the outset. By dictating *how* things are to be done you are taking on a feminine role and essentially crippling one of her innate talents, resulting in reducing her power and fulfillment as a woman. Just as men have a desire to express their leadership qualities women have a desire to express their strategic prowess. Failure to recognize this fact may cause major issues in our personal development and ability to sustain fulfilling relationships.

What is the Reason?

Our ability to reason is a prerequisite to us making the best choices in our lives. Reasoning is our ability to accurately define our reality. It is our ability to be reasonable in our assessment of what is being presented to us. In order to be reasonable, we must be rational where rationality says to assign qualities to things based upon their merit and not our personal biases, emotional attachments, or something's potential.

Saying that, metaphysically, masculinity is an external trait and femininity is an internal trait, means men oftentimes tend to be externally focused on their physical surroundings; thus we are thinking deeply about their qualities. This is different than thinking about the potential of a thing, which is classified as a feminine trait. So from this standpoint, I am classifying reasoning as a masculine trait, because the ability to reason requires that you call it like you *see* it, as opposed to what it *could* be. Fear of loss cannot enter the equation, nor can attachments to material things be a variable in our assessment. The hope of what may be or the potential of a person or thing is not a part of the reasoning process. Giving individuals a second chance or how you feel about the situation at that particular time has nothing to do with reasoning. You have to call it like you see it and if you do not like what you see, change it rather than hope it changes on its own or as a result of someone else's efforts. That is what defines a man and a leader—one who sets things right. So whatever your idea of "right" is, the goal is to look at things reasonably and rationally and fix what needs fixing, rather than hoping and praying they will be all right in the end. Leave the prayers and faith (symbolized by the eyes being closed, thus a feminine trait) to someone else. As the man in the situation you need to take action (symbolized by keeping the eyes open).

Note: That being said, men should not discount the power of faith and prayer as those mental abilities have the same potential to affect our physical environment as direct physical confrontation. They are two sides of the same coin. All we are saying is that when you, as a man, take direct physical action, it strengthens your overall masculine nature and will be helpful in balancing your personal health and relationships.

Our Best Assets are Our People

Two of the most underrated and unrecognized qualities of leadership are the responsibilities to empower the people around you to be successful in every aspect of their lives, not just to teach them new skills, but to help them find themselves while educating them and at the same time to strengthen their minds, bodies, and spirits by showing them how to conquer their environments as they learn to master their emotions. Most people choose to follow a leader to get the benefit of growing into their fullness as they prepare to take on new challenges and face life. That is the true leader-follower tradeoff. In place of receiving a salary, having a fear of being fired, or you being a dependent and they the guardian, it is about an actual exchange of value between people and what a leader offers. These are those intangible, intrinsic experiences and lessons that cannot be bought over the counter.

One of my fondest recollections of being a part of a spiritual community and organization was of the men being called on to do tons of work on a volunteer basis, wherein oftentimes the work required very late nights and significant physical labor. One of the attractions to doing the work was the fellowship and camaraderie among men, but the most appealing part for me was being around some of the older and wiser male leaders. It was like being in a classroom setting and learning all about life and its secrets. I could ask questions or just listen to the stories being told and felt each time I would come away a better person. You always knew these leaders had your best interests at heart no matter what was happening. I just wanted to do good by them because I considered them so valuable and necessary to my life; I can honestly say I learned more about being a man, husband, and father during those years than in any other part of my life.

As men our responsibility is to empower our entire families, both immediate and extended, as a unit and as individuals. That is what is meant by a man needing to be in the home to correctly raise the children, especially boys, although it goes beyond boys and children extending to wives as well. It is a matter of having someone there with the skills and interest to support us in our growth as human beings. To let us know where we are right now, as opposed to where we could be (potential), based on our individual goals, and helping us get there.

Romance with No Finance is a Nuisance

Our ability to extract the resources we need for ourselves and our family is an indication of our level of mastery over our environment. How can we lead anyone unless we have shown a level of mastery over our environment? This is not about being rich, but being resourceful. Additionally, and most important, is the recognition that resources are needed to advance life and prioritizing their attainment is crucial. The attainment of resources primarily falls under the Negotiator masculine trait and is discussed later.

Organizing

If there is anything a leader can do, it is organize people and resources to accomplish an objective. That is really their most important contribution; identify the right people to get the job done and giving them what they need to be successful. The key here is that they are implementing a plan authored by someone else. Remember, strategic planning is not a leader's core competency, but implementation is. You may have heard some of the top CEO's say that if you can run one business, you can run any business. Well it is true because organizational ability transcends industry, market conditions, competition, economic climate, and the like.

The same holds true with running and organizing your family. It is the leadership and organizational skills that are important, instead of which woman you happen to be with. That is why some men can keep ten women happy and others have issues with one.

Transparency

It is important that the people you are leading know you are being truthful, honest, and sincere in your efforts to lead them. There should never be a case in which side deals are being cut for one's own personal benefit or at the expense of the group. Transparency does not mean that you reveal all your secrets, strengths, and deficits, but that you are open and honest with your intentions.

Clarifying Leadership Notes

Consider these notes as things to be mindful of as you embark upon your leadership journey.

Note #1: Leadership is not wisdom. Remember that leaders call it like they see it, which leaves little time to think deeply about all the possibilities that exist; leave that to your gurus. A leader has an understanding analogous to the part of the iceberg above the water, but wisdom understands the part of the iceberg below the surface, too.

Note #2: Leaders do not do, they lead and direct. Get the right people, give them what they need, and get out of the way. A leader's job is to find the right people to do the job, not do the job himself. As a leader, if you are getting involved in doing a specific task, you have compromised the effectiveness of your organization and family. If your wife needs support to take care of her responsibilities then find it for her; however, taking over her responsibilities yourself is not the best solution.

Note #3: Leaders are not in charge of the relationship or the family, but do have specific responsibilities within the relationship or family unit. Women, specifically the Devotee personality type in women, have the other half of the leadership type responsibilities in the family. The masculine leadership trait is best suited to manage what is known and logical; whereas, the feminine leadership trait is best suited to manage situations with numerous unknowns or ones that are chaotic or unorthodox in nature. Another way to say this is that men will manage the implementation of the plan and the women can manage the formulation of the plan. This fact needs to be acknowledged because in a moment of arrogance, leaders tend to think they are running the whole show, which is far from the case and in the long run will definitely lead to a breakdown in the relationship.

Benefits and Affects to the Feminine Traits in Women: A man living proficiently as a Leader will assist his wife's ability to come into her Devotee personality by feeling cared for and prioritized; thus enabling her see a positive future for the relationship and family. This positive outlook will strengthen the bond between you and your wife. It will also further strengthen her Visionary personality enabling her to be more creative and generate ideas that can benefit the family.

Leader Self-Test

The following questions measure certain leadership qualities required for a successful relationship, so answer the questions honestly. Your result total will give you insights into the leadership developmental processes best suited for you.

Leader Self-Test Questions

#	Question	Considerations	Score
1.	Are you accountable to anyone other than yourself for how you function in your relationship? Accountable to someone means they have authority to openly critique how you function in the relationship AND you have enough respect for them where their input may influence your behavior.	0 persons = 0 1 person = 1 2 or more = 2	
2.	What percent of plans do you implement based upon your wife's direct guidance and input? In other words, when she tells you *how* to accomplish something, how often do you listen and follow? *Note: If your wife is not offering her opinion on how to accomplish things, then zero points are earned. There may be an issue around suppression of her input, which is a larger*	Less than 50% = 0 Greater than or equal to 50% = 1 Greater than 75% = 2	

	problem.		
3.	Do you anticipate and resolve issues before or as soon as they come up? Resolution means the issue has been addressed in full and everyone is clear on what to do next, not that the problem has been completely solved.	If 90% of the time or more = 1 Less than 90% of the time = 0	
4.	Do you promote building your wife's and children's skills, capabilities, and overall personal development? This includes putting them in the best environment to be successful in their lives.	If 90% of the time or more = 1 If less than 90% of the time = 0	
		Your Total Earned	
		Total Possible	6

Leader Self Test Rating Summary
6 out of 6 – Proficient
5 out of 6 – Good
4 out of 6 – Needs Improvement
3 out of 6 – Seriously Deficient
0-2 out of 6 – Complete Leader Character Void

Developmental Processes: The Leader

These developmental processes are practical exercises any man can use to strengthen their own Leader masculine traits. The following exercises will develop the talents of being present and making proper choices.

Leader Developmental Process #1:

One of the most important aspects of being a leader is your awareness of your surroundings so that you always know what is going on around you. The first exercise is to observe your wife and document five things about her external appearance and mood. External appearance includes her size, weight, hair, makeup, facial expressions (as a mood indication), walk, and so forth. Mood observations would include things like if she was happy or sad, relaxed or ready for intimacy, or maybe needing some attention.

This exercise requires that you spend a few extra moments observing her and then a few additional moments documenting (at least mentally) what you have observed. This will allow you to consider what your observations mean and, if any action is required, to provide healing or attention if necessary.

This exercise also can be applied when you enter a room or as you are driving. Getting in the habit of noticing details of your surroundings will teach you to be present with your environment, rather than floating through your day. What you should observe are certain details that are important and informative that you may tend to overlook. Let's rediscover the subtleties of our wives and our surroundings.

Leader Developmental Process #2:

Another leadership trait is the ability to make choices and stick with them. This builds trust and stability among those looking to you for guidance. For this exercise, pick a personal bad habit and then think of the corrective behavior for it. For example, if you are trying to lose weight or are watching your health and should not eat sweets, choose not to eat sweets. When the urge comes up or when you walk by a sweet shop, make the choice to pick an alternative food source to satisfy the craving. During the exercise, take notice of the justifications that you give yourself to have a slice of chocolate cake (or whatever your sweet craving is) despite the fact that you know it is not the best thing for you at the time. Also notice the internal pangs that you feel during the struggle to make this different or uncomfortable choice. It is important to note that these feelings are the types of emotional responses that tend to hold us back from making true progress in certain areas of our lives, including our relationships. It is apparent that there are choices we will need to make in our relationships that are not going to be our favorite things to do, but nonetheless need to be done in order to create harmony and help move things forward. This exercise will give the required practice in moving beyond the internal blocks that make the difficult choices tough to make.

Chapter 9:
Masculine Trait #3: The Soldier

"This is what I believe and I'm willing to die for it;
period!" – Will Smith

I always used to say that my wife never really appreciated me unless I was in some sort of pain. I know that sounds crazy, but I got to a point where I really believed it. But as time went on, I rationalized her behavior to be like that of people who are in pain and have a tendency to transfer their pain to others for relief, much like a mother holding her son after he had scraped his knee. The mother is in some way absorbing the hurt her son feels, and he understands this intuitively, which is why children will search for their mothers first when they get hurt; take the pain away please.

In my younger days while growing up, I had a general feeling about women—if a man is not going out of his way to do or provide for her than she won't feel secure with you as a man. She may appreciate the gesture, but it won't make her feel safe with you. But now that I am older, more mature and experienced, I realize that my notion was, in fact, true and not just a figment of my imagination, which brings us to our discussion of the Soldier.

We all realize that a soldier is someone who puts his or her body, health, and well being on the line for others or a cause. Soldiers are all about self-sacrifice. If the general gives the command to dive on a land mine, it's done without question. Taking that course of action would not be appealing to most people; however, because of the outcome of such a selfless action, it would be greatly appreciated by all who would benefit from it—especially women. The Soldier is a masculine personality trait and consciousness and one that women must experience to feel secure, protected, and prioritized. When women are in the presence of a soldier, they tend to be more relaxed, which translates into them moving into their natural feminine energy.

Let's take a moment to add some context to this discussion. A major challenge that men have in relationships is women not feeling secured and protected by them. In other words, you haven't set up an environment and a mode of functioning with her that allows her to relax. Often times a woman's primary concern is whether or not you as the man will be there over the long term and while you're there successfully promoting and protecting her well being.

A woman's insecurity can breed uncertainty, which can cause her worry and stress. Once stress sets in, the relationship is functioning at a deficit, and the existing tension can become a breeding ground for other issues. If your wife is stressed, you can count on disruption in the home or relationship. A prime example would be problems in your sex life. The bottom line is this, when women feel secure, they are more within their natural feminine energy, which causes them to become moister and more orgasmic during sex. This, of course, is a good thing and anything contrary can lead to further issues. But, on the other hand, a non-orgasmic woman who is not receiving pleasure during sex will bring a whole different set of challenges to the relationship. So from this example you can see the domino effect and results caused by our inability as men to step up and provide our women security in our relationships.

As men it is critical that we make personal sacrifices for the sake of the women in our lives. From one perspective, this can be viewed as the damsel in distress scenario in which the man nearly dies to save the woman from sure demise. I know this sounds old fashioned, but there is a strong subconscious communication made when a man sacrifices for a woman. This is how we develop a true connection. This action also increases our

81

confidence, which gets the testosterone flowing, which resonates into every area of the relationship, including sexually.

The Soldier's sacrifice is not only for his wife and family, but also for his goals and objectives as well. It is critical that men make this same personal sacrifice to achieve greatness in the world or at least make their mark. This is important for our women and children to see, as it adds to their feelings of security. You are communicating that you are a no-nonsense individual who knows what he wants and is willing to sacrifice for it. It also communicates that if you have chosen to be with this woman, it is for a good reason and not about playing games.

Being a soldier replaces the need for excessive displays of love through materialistic expressions. Buying gifts for your wife is only one form of sacrifice, but men oftentimes find themselves in an endless loop of trying to buy the world as a display of love. The challenge is that although women like and appreciate material expressions of love, it does not touch the very core of their being; it is like putting a bandage on a broken leg.

Some practical examples of being the Soldier include minimizing your wife's exposure to the undesirable elements of the outside world. For example, holding the car door open for her, ensuring she doesn't get wet in the rain, holding her arm while she is walking, ensuring she is walking on the inside of the sidewalk and sitting on the inside of the booth at a restaurant, getting the groceries out of the car, filling the gas tank, driving the car, helping her put her coat on, carrying her bags (not purse), ordering her food, answering the home phone, answering the door, driving her to work, picking her up from work, being the last one to bed and ensuring everything is locked and secured, maintaining order with the children, ensuring she is satisfied sexually first and foremost, helping her relax when she's tired, holding her at night before she sleeps, and the list goes on. From one perspective these are your standard chivalrous deeds, but they shouldn't be underestimated and they should be done consistently. More importantly than the deeds themselves is having a Soldier's state of mind and presence, which will help your wife and family feel secure. It's having a protective disposition in all you do with her as if you were guarding a delicate flower. It's a fiery and dry presence that will help your wife stay calm, relaxed, moist, and supple.

Speaking of moist, the Soldier duties extend to the bedroom as well. As a man you should be prepared to do the work to activate the pleasure centers with your wife. This includes sacrificing your short-term pleasure in deference to both of your long-term extended and more intense and fulfilling pleasures. As the man you need to facilitate the sexual interaction between you and your wife and make all the required sacrifices along the way, which includes maintaining certain sexual positions, as well as a consistent rhythmic pace when necessary. Sometimes sex can be tiring and uncomfortable for a man; especially when we prioritize her pleasure, but this is the sacrifice we are talking about.

Benefits and Affects to the Feminine Traits in Women: Living proficiently as a Soldier will assist your wife in feeling safe and secure thus coming into her Conservationist personality and enabling her to properly care for herself, her family, and environment. This security will help her respect you as a man and improve her willingness to follow you and take risks. It will also begin improve her Lover personality enabling her to feel more secure in expressing her true personality and sexual nature both in and out of the bedroom.

Soldier Self-Test

The question below will measure your overall effectiveness as a soldier, so answer it honestly.

Soldier Self-Test Questions

#	Question	Considerations	Score
1.	Do you regularly (often as required) sacrifice your comfort, wants, desires, and personal plans to address an issue with your significant other, wife/girlfriend, etc.? Some examples include not going to the game if she is going through emotional hardship, or not going to sleep if there is something on her mind, or canceling plans to hang with the guys to address an emotional or spiritual challenge she is having, or work a job you do not like so that the family has the money required to live, or putting off your short-term pleasure during sex to ensure her pleasure, etc.	If 90% of the time or more = 1 If less than 90% of the time = 0	
		Your Total Earned	
		Total Possible	1

Soldier Self-Test Rating Summary

1 out of 1 – Proficient
0 out of 1 – Complete Soldier Character Void

Developmental Processes: The Soldier

The developmental processes are practical exercises any man can use to strengthen the Soldier masculine trait. The following exercises will develop the talents of being fearless and selfless.

Soldier Developmental Process #1:

In this exercise you must identify at least three of your fears and prepare to face them. Allow me to offer some assistance here for those men who think they do not have any fears. Sure you can walk down into the basement with no lights on (most of you) or even kill a snake in the garden, but let's not overlook the not-so-obvious things like visiting the in-laws, talking to your children about sex, confessing a lie to your wife or friend, telling your boss what you really think about the job he or she is doing, talking to a woman in the club, confronting your mother about some issues from your childhood that are still affecting you today, dedicating yourself to self-improvement (i.e. losing weight, getting in shape, going back to school, developing your skills beyond your comfort zone, etc.) or whatever issues you have difficulty confronting or engaging. Trust me; you do have some fears, so spend as much time as you need thinking long and hard on this one. Once you have identified your fears, your next job is to walk through them. Do what it is you have always feared to do with no fear at all. The key here is not thinking about the negative consequences, but instead knowing you will be fine in the end. Remember fear is simply the mental projection and visualization of undesirable future outcomes.

Soldier Developmental Process #2:

The second major theme of the soldier personality is selflessness. For this exercise you must identify someone in need and give your time, energy, and resources to help them. The greater the sacrifice, the more effective this process will be. It will also help if you pick a situation you are not necessarily comfortable with. You can measure a selfless act by the amount of pain and discomfort it brings to you personally. Giving to a charity counts when its not necessarily something you want to do at that time or may delay a personal project, but it doesn't count when it's something you do regularly and primarily for a tax break. In other words, doing something to ease your conscience or gain a benefit is not a selfless act. If you can't think of a scenario where others may need help on their terms and not yours, fear not; it will be presented to you as long as you open yourself up to that possibility.

Chapter 10:
Masculine Trait #4: The Negotiator

"…when someone asks if you're a God, you say 'Yes'!" –
Winston Zeddemore, Ghost Busters™

It is important to understand that women appreciate communication and reassurance. It helps them come into a higher aspect of their femininity; namely, what I call their Lover feminine trait. Let me add the appropriate level of criticality to that statement—proper and consistent "over-communication" is crucial to a healthy relationship because it ensures you and your wife are in synch at all times; thus minimizing worry and stress – imagining the worst outcomes.

I experienced this the most while working for women when I was a consultant in the information technology field. It seemed as though they had the over-communicate golden rule. I had never before sent so many e-mails per day, which explained the obvious about what had already been agreed upon, the confirming and reconfirming of expectations, the fact that an agreement had been reached on certain milestones and deliverables, or the fact that I will be out of the office for two hours on Friday and back online by 3:00 p.m. Classic stuff.

The mindset of the men I worked for was more like: just get it done and take 360 degrees of accountability for it, you can send one hundred e-mails or one, it is all on you; just show up at the agreed upon time with the agreed upon deliverables and only call me in emergencies. Okay, so I may be exaggerating a bit, but I know you can see and understand the difference. In your relationships it should be the same thing; communicate regularly and with relevant information.

Why is this communication necessary? As I stated earlier, women tend to think broadly, which means they are constantly reviewing scenarios and possibilities in their minds and may have a tendency to lose touch with the present reality. You can tell when this happens because is manifests as worry and fear and eventually stress, tension, and illness. Remember that the feminine modality of thinking is around possibilities, whereas the masculine modality of thinking is around actuality. Another way to say this is men think about the present and women tend to think about the future. A simpler way to state it is that men live in the present, and women live in the past and future. I know it can get confusing, but not knowing the distinction between the masculine and feminine roles is why couples tend to argue about events that have taken place during different points in time, which usually makes their arguments pointless because men and women tend to experience reality differently. For example, because women tend to live in the past more than men, they tend to have better memories and can recall events in their finest detail so really the argument is over before it got started.

It should be noted that communicating is not only for you to share your plans to your wife, but also to find out her plans as well. My wife is notorious for committing us to events without my input or approval, and I may not find out about it until that day. It could be an event with forty people or a special night just for us; the magnitude of the event or occasion really doesn't matter. The first step of growth for me was to be at peace whenever she did this and honor it as if the event had been on my calendar for a month, especially since it is not like these were not good ideas. It is just that I was not in the loop until the last minute even though in her mind we had discussed it extensively. The second thing I had to do was take responsibility for not knowing in the first place. The bottom line is that if I had spent the right amount of quality time with her everyday, these "opportunities" would naturally come to the forefront during our conversations when I would ask her, "So, do you have any plans for the weekend?"

"Oh, yeah, we're going to a black tie affair on Saturday night, it should be fun."

"Sweet! Glad I asked." (*I would say that last sentence to myself.*)

Men in their masculine personality can naturally verbally communicate ideas in a logical format and can effectively communicate their intentions to their wives and others. Metaphysically, this translates into describing the physical phenomena occurring all around us. Women in their full feminine personalities have a stronger ability to communicate subtle phenomena, which is why they are better at explaining their emotions and feelings–things which are seemingly intangible. We will discuss this more in later chapters.

When I say men have a stronger aptitude for verbal communication around specific physical phenomena, it does not translate into being more intelligent or smarter. Please do not fall into that trap.

Remember our rule is always 50/50 regarding what men and women bring to the table in relationships. That applies to physical and mental ability, intelligence, resilience, emotionality, inherent skills and talents, and so forth. It is simply the application and form of the expression of these talents that tends to be different.

Verbal and written communications are simply forms of expression; how we use them to describe life is what differentiates the masculine and feminine modalities. As men, our talent and role is to communicate very specific states of reality to our wives in such a manner that there is no doubt of what is being said or going on here in the present.

Oftentimes when women are disheartened in a relationship, it is because they have not been reassured that they are the priority in their man's life. This should not be taken lightly, as a man can only focus on a few things at any one time with great effectiveness; thus the reminders from our women, that there are areas of our lives needing our attention, are justified and appropriate.

Looking at this a bit closer, another primary reason it is critical to communicate with our wives is because they have a tendency to live in their minds and be oblivious to their physical surroundings. The result is a need for someone to communicate consistently what is happening physically around them. Remember, it is the leadership personality trait that understands our physical surroundings, including people and their true motives, the economic climate, and so forth. This is why leaders are followed; they can see something everyone else cannot. The man in a relationship must provide this special sight capability, or else the relationship will encounter obstacles along the way. If we look at most relationship scenarios, it is the woman who is seeking reassurance from her man. She is the one that wants to know if you love her, care for her, and will never leave her. What happens during a breakup? The first thing she may say is, "You said you loved me and that we would always be together," and she is justified in saying this because it is a woman's nature to take what you say and do and create her reality with it; it is all she has to go on. Why? Because seeing things for what they are is not a feminine trait. That is the job of the Leader. So in essence communication is a necessity for her. She wants to hear from you how you feel about her and the relationship as opposed to simply observing your actions and drawing a conclusion.

During my years in corporate America, I worked with and for a number of women. I actually had more female managers than male over the course of my career and the consistent attribute of my female managers was their need for me to over-communicate. This meant providing constant, real-time status on what was happening on the project and with my direct reports. I remember thinking it was complete overkill and that I would go nuts trying to meet their communication requirements. One of my managers used to tell me when I did not respond fast enough to e-mails (within an hour or so) people start to think something is wrong. I just remember thinking that could be the cause for such inefficiency on the projects—people were responding so quickly it was hard to believe they have thought through the situation and done the required research and due diligence—a lot of people talking, but little true substance. When I started adopting these practices, I remember feeling more like a busybody, as opposed to someone who was solution oriented. It was as if my value was being measured by how fast I could identify an issue and notify a broader audience. The solution would be to call a meeting, which could only be quasi effective because everyone would be multitasking and not focusing on the subject at hand anyway. It was always interesting to hear how many times people had to repeat a question because folks just were not mentally present in the conversation or how many times someone would try to answer a question they did not hear because they were instant messaging another coworker. The point here is not to solve corporate inefficiencies, but to drive home the point that men and women have different tendencies concerning communication requirements.

One of my female co-workers, who was my peer manager with me on the same project, used to criticize me for not reading every e-mail that came through my inbox so I was not up on the latest happenings with the team and on the project. Not only was this not my dominant tendency, but also I knew she would keep me informed of the major happenings and communicate to me the details I needed to know. I would kind of use her as my e-mail notification system and reader. Conversely, my impression was she would use me, too, for my deep, thought-out opinions on certain matters, so it all worked well in the end. She would make sure all issues and risks were identified and categorized, and I would develop solutions to the key ones most impacting the project. From that standpoint we made a great team.

The male managers I worked for did not expect to hear from me every day, and if they did hear from me, they thought there must be an issue or problem. But not only that, they had other ways of keeping tabs on me, like observing my work as it unfolded and through discussions with others.

Lastly, in relationships it's important to understand that communication is not only about status or whereabouts, but reaffirming the reality you want for you family. Things like reaffirming your wife's beauty as she works to maintain herself and make improvements is key. Reaffirming the reasons you are with her and your expectations of your future together are critical for her and the relationship. She will take your words and build a picture of the future. That is a key feminine talent; creating mental images of the future and facilitating their manifestation.

Benefits and Affects to the Feminine Traits in Women: Living proficiently as a Negotiator will assist your wife's ability to come into her full true Lover personality by feeling adored and loved; thus enabling her to express her sexuality and full sensual nature everywhere she goes. As a result she will feel more attractive and beautiful to you and in general. It will also further strengthen her Conservationist personality enabling her to cherish and appreciate what she has and all you have to offer.

Negotiator Self-Test

The following questions will measure your skills and development as a Negotiator, so answer them honestly.

Negotiator Self-Test Questions

#	Question	Considerations	Score
1.	When talking to and about your wife and family do you promote their highest good and potential at all times?	Yes (all the time) = 1 No (some of the time) = 0	
2.	Do you form relationships with other people for the sole purpose of obtaining the resources required for you and your family? In other words, do you have a resource network that can be leveraged to obtain tangible resources?	Yes = 1 No = 0	
3.	Do you feel confident interacting with others in any social or business environment that you may find yourself in?	Yes = 1 No = 0	
4.	Do you actively communicate what you're doing, where you're going, how you're feeling, and what the overall status and condition of important	If 90% of the time or more = 1 If less than 90% of the time = 0	

	happenings are? Do you reinforce to your wife and family that everything is going to be okay regardless of how things may look at the time?		
		Your Total Earned	
		Total Possible	4

Negotiator Self-Test Rating Summary

4 out of 4 – Proficient
3 out of 4 – Good
2 out of 4 – Needs Improvement
1 or 0 out of 4 – Complete Negotiator Character Void

Developmental Processes: Negotiator

The developmental processes are practical exercises any man can use to strengthen the Negotiator masculine traits within him. The following exercises will develop the talents of promotion and negotiation.

Negotiator Developmental Process #1:

This process will help develop your promotion skills, particularly, promoting yourself. Choose an event to attend for which you do not have any contacts, friends, or associates and initiate conversation with at least twenty people you don't know (not at one time, of course). During the conversations, your goal is to sell your highest self to each person you are talking to. Your highest self is a projection of where you want to be, as opposed to where you actually are at this time. ***Note:*** *If you are already where you want to be, then go with that.*

For example, let's say you want to become an entrepreneur and you have been doing work to develop a service offering, but are still in a nine-to-five job. At this event, talk only of your entrepreneurial business and make no mention of your nine-to-five job. If someone explicitly asks you about your day job versus if you are in business for yourself full time, you have to decide where you want to be. This is called a crossroads situation where you need to choose who you are now. Remember, there is no past or future, but only your now. So if in your mind you are working a nine-to-five, that is what you are doing and you will continue to attract things into your life that will support you in working that job. If in your mind you are a full-time entrepreneur, that is what you are; thus you are attracting circumstances to support that scenario as well. Not only will you attract circumstances to support that reality, but you will also act the part by spending your time on tasks and activities that support your business. This is how we create our lives.

Negotiator Developmental Process #2:

This process will help you develop your negotiation skills. Think of something that you want—it could be a car, a new suit, a date with a woman you have a crush on, a ticket to a concert, someone to help you with a project, getting into the club for free, etc. Next select a price or a level of exchange you are willing to accommodate to obtain it. For example, if you want a new car and the car costs $49,999 and requires five percent down, plus tags and title, your goal will be to pick a price say of $43,999, zero down, plus tags and title. Your objective is to secure the car at the price you want to pay in exchange for what you are willing to offer. The objective is also to negotiate with integrity and offer something of value, which in this case is a sale to a solid customer who will buy today, maintain payments, and get regular maintenance through the dealership, as well as justification and proof of why the car is only worth what you're offering. Maybe that same dealership was offering discounts two months ago which ultimately brought the price close to your price, etc. Don't offer something you don't have, like an 850 credit score or a car exchange rate of twenty thousand dollars if your current car is only worth eight grand. This is just one example, but the point is to learn to communicate with others while offering something of value in exchange for what you want. This exercise will also help you appreciate the value of what you already own. Often times we undervalue ourselves and our assets, thus we end up paying more than required for services, favors, and goodwill from others.

Chapter 11:
The Fifth Masculine-Feminine Trait

"We are unified with everything in the Universe by a single undifferentiated consciousness that permeates all things and all parts of our being." – Rakhem Seku

We have discussed four masculine character traits, but there is one other trait inherent equally in both men and women: the Peacekeeper. The Peacekeeper is that part of us that is willing to assume whatever position or character required to bring harmony and unity to any situation. The Peacekeeper is interested in the highest good in all situations and represents a common thread that binds all human beings together and also gives us a common perspective on life. This is important because the masculine and feminine perspectives can be in perfect synchronicity when the Peacekeeper is accessed by all parties involved.

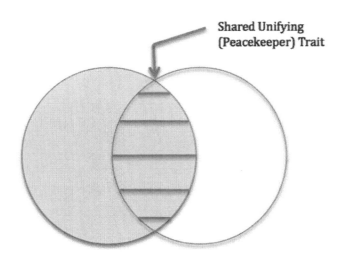

Shared Unifying
(Peacekeeper) Trait

That said, it's important to note that the Peacekeeper part of our being is a separate trait apart from our masculine and feminine traits. In other words, it's not a combination of the masculine and feminine, but is that from which the masculine and feminine are born. It is our essential unifying nature as human beings and manifests itself exactly the same in all people. So when it's said that "we are all one," the Peacekeeper part of our beings are the physical and mental manifestation of that truth in all of us.

Chapter 12:
Dispelling the Commitment Myth

"Honor is to a man what commitment is to a woman." –
Rakhem Seku

– commitment.
"2c : the state or an instance of being obligated or
emotionally impelled <a commitment to a cause>"
(2010). Merriam-Webster Online Dictionary.

I have often heard that a major masculine trait (and one that all men should have) is the ability to commit. I disagree. Commitment is a feminine trait. Men don't really understand commitment. It is against our very nature to stay committed to any one idea or thing over a period of time. We naturally reevaluate our circumstances to ensure we are headed in the right direction. If you want to find the best examples of commitment, you need to study the women around you. Commitment is the woman who stands by her son no matter what he does in society. Commitment is refusing to let go of someone even though they are dead and gone and continuing to carrying that memory with you everywhere you go. Men will feel compelled to leave a relationship, whether intimate or business, in a minute, if it violates what it was originally set out to be. Honoring agreements is our nature.

In football if the coach says he will commit to the run for the rest of the game, but it is third and fifteen and the defense has eleven men in the box and getting the first down guarantees the win, will he stay committed? Hell no. Play action fake and hit the tight end for a twenty-yard pass down the middle. However, true commitment says you don't abandon the run under any circumstances; staying the course regardless of the changing environmental factors. Trust me; he will stay committed until it is no longer makes sense to do so. Is a coach committed to winning every game? No way. Not if it means his star players may get hurt or if it locks him into a contract instead of having the option to make twice the money somewhere else. Oh, so he is committed to winning the championship game? Maybe he is or maybe he isn't. It depends upon his relationship to the owner, the year of his contract, and a slew of other factors.

Men in their masculine personality are loyal and honorable, which is separate from being committed. Loyalty means I will follow through with my word and not leave you out to dry provided you hold up your end of the bargain and support me throughout the process just as we agreed. It's a contract, meaning I will do it because I said so, not because I necessarily believe in you or the ideas you are presenting. If a better idea comes along, I may want to pursue that one instead, but I will do the honorable thing and exit our contract according to the protocols to which we have agreed. Why stay committed to something that is no longer useful, especially if it may result in severe harm or death?

This had to be said because men are often accused of not committing to a relationship when, in fact, the bottom line is *that's not our job.* Our job and duty is to honor the relationship based upon a mutual understanding of why we came together in the first place. We are honoring the commitment our wives are making to our relationship and us as men; we are not committing to the relationship itself. Our expression of love is not a promise to be with women under any and all circumstances. There's a subconscious feeling of betrayal that comes up in men when we sense the contract has changed and shifted or that our wives are not honoring their end of the relationship agreement. This is why so many men do not get married, but rather choose to stay single; they just do not see that women will be able to uphold their end of the bargain over the long haul. Men's thoughts are yes, it is clear that she is committed to having a baby and being in *a* marriage, but what does that have to do with me? She has not differentiated me from any other man on the planet, and that is problematic. She has not committed to me and my journey and my individual growth so how can I truly honor her? The only way a man really feels comfortable being with a woman long-term is if she is

103

truly committed to *him*, which is a big difference from being committed to a relationship or the concept of marriage. Unfortunately, most women are not committed to the men they are with; therefore, they never get the maximum benefit from them, but spend a lot of time complaining about it nonetheless. Men can sense a mile away when women are committed only to the relationship itself. When we sense a woman is committed to us, we will *choose* to love that woman for all time.

How do we know that a woman is committed to us? It's how she places you in her life. Are you her Monk, Leader, Soldier, and Negotiator or are you a placeholder for the concept of marriage, relationships, and children. Does she respect you and your opinion? Does she give you the opportunity to grow, to fail, to dream, to provide for her and the family or does she challenge ever word you say? Does she falsely tell you she has no other attractions other than to you to make you feel comfortable or is she honest and forthright? Does she let you know the uniqueness she honors in you? There is much more to this discussion with respect to the feminine nature, but it is covered in my wife's book *Change Your Man*. My message in this book is primarily for the men.

Chapter 13:
Dealing with Conflict

"Everything serves to further." – I Ching

Our goal is to evolve into our highest self so that we may pass our greatest gifts on to our children, wives and mates, and communities. As we work through the content of this book to improve our effectiveness as men, which consequently improves our relationships, let's keep our heads in reality. The probability of the two complementing energies (masculine and feminine) and each one's perspectives coming into conflict will remain high for a time. When these conflicts arise, we should address them so that we have the highest chance of resolution.

The Language of Love

The premise of this book is that men are equal, but different from women. Additionally, because men and women are both earthly beings, their every action falls under earthly law (e.g. the laws of physics, time and space, etc.), which means they are mathematical in nature. If this is true, every action has a corresponding number assigned to it, so taking it a step further, a female action plus a male action equals a result. I know what I say tends to sound somewhat technical at times, but essentially it means we can take an unbalanced or negative action and diffuse it with the correct positive action. In other words, an extreme negative action plus an extreme positive action equals harmony, balance, and peace.

In my last book, *The BaGau Character Map: Science, Analysis, and Interpretation,* I stated there are only nine primary numbers in the world representing the nine primary universal laws. All other numbers are a combination of the original nine. So why is all of this important? It is important because men have demonstrated a poor track record in understanding how women communicate. In the *BaGau Character Map: Science, Analysis, and Interpretation*, I have reduced women's communication to mathematical formulas to help us understand the required masculine response for specific feminine behavior easier to figure out. Look at it as a cheat sheet of sorts.

Here is how it works. For each of the four feminine character traits there are a set of unbalanced or negative, emotional behaviors a woman may tend to display throughout a relationship. They are as follows:

Feminine Character Traits	Unbalanced (Negative) Emotional Response
Devotee (The Mother)	Worry, Stress
Conservationist	Selfishness, Depression, Greed
Lover	Unattractiveness, Neediness
Visionary	Doubtful, Not Trusting

Here is the trick. When a woman is experiencing one of the above emotions, it may look like something entirely different. As a matter of fact, it almost always does. For example, worry may appear as your wife being verbally confrontational with you or bucking against your every suggestion as opposed to her sitting in the corner biting her fingernails. The verbal confrontation might be her way of saying she is uncomfortable with how things are going. An example of feeling unattractive may be her not wanting to go out to an event or not wanting any company over to the house. It's not necessarily her being antisocial, but rather her not feeling her best. So the thing to be aware of here is to take your time in assessing which emotional response is applicable in the situation.

We also want to be aware of the "communication vehicle," which is *how* she communicates what she is feeling. Oftentimes we confuse the communication vehicle for the emotion the woman is experiencing. The following are the communication vehicles:

Communication Vehicle	Masculine v. Feminine
Direct Verbal	Masculine
Indirect Verbal	Feminine
Direct Action	Masculine
Indirect Action	Feminine

Remember, direct verbal communication is a masculine trait, so when women are expressing themselves, you may have to go through a few layers of communication to get to the essence of the situation. What that means for you is that you may have to apply the Behavior Response methods in the table below more than once to get to the real issue.

The matrix below details some common unbalanced feminine behaviors that can potentially lead to conflict and the corresponding required male responses to restore balance.

The unbalanced feminine behaviors (numbered 1, 2, 3, etc.) match the same male balancing number in the next column.

Masculine Behavior Response Matrix

Unbalanced Feminine Behavior	Balancing Masculine Behavior
Devotee	**Leader**
1. Overly emotional, manifesting as crying, jealousy, and all mental and internal thought processing that cause stress. *Note: No external violence in this particular scenario.*	1. As soon as the emotionalism is identified, immediately confront her to find out the source of the issue. This may require that he hug and embrace her to show he is present and can be trusted with her feelings and well being. Connecting with her on a sexual level helps to reinforce your presence with her. *Note: The holding also helps disperse and absorb any tension she may be going through.*
2. Condescending behavior in the form of argumentative communication. This is mental and emotional abuse by which the goal is to influence a man's actions by creating mental instability.	2. Confront her about her reasons for arguing and confronting you. Hug and embrace her to show her that you are present with her and that arguing is not required for her to communicate with you. Connecting with her on a sexual level helps to reinforce your presence with her.

Conservationist	Soldier
1. Depression. Physically or mentally dangerous to one's own well being by creating and reacting to mental scenarios which are not true.	1. If she is depressed spend as much time as required to bring her back into balance. This is a sacrifice of time and comfort and requires him to be physically and emotionally present. He must physically and mentally be with her for as long as required and reassure her that everything will be all right. If she is in danger of harming herself emotionally, he must be with her and ensure she is safe or seek outside help.
2. Overly conservative in not allowing you to take chances and risks as a man.	2. When she does not allow you to take risks and make sacrifices, you must make sacrifices on her behalf until she is comfortable with the necessity and benefit of risk taking in general. Once she has received benefits from this behavior, she will be more willing to allow risk taking in general. *Note: Complete comfort from her is not a requirement for a man to do what he must on behalf of the family. The same holds true for those things that she must do as well.*

Lover	Negotiator
1. Does not feel she is beautiful and attractive.	1. Communicate to her that she is beautiful, and show her through gifts and public displays of adornment.
2. Needs excessive sexual attention to feel whole.	2. Same as above. Connecting with her on a sexual level helps to reinforce her powers of attraction, thus reinforcing her beauty inside and out.
Visionary	**Monk**
1. Wants excessive sex.	1. Help her understand her deeper purpose in life. Show her the power that resides within. You must also master tantric and other techniques around sex and intimacy so that each sexual encounter with her is deep, meaningful, and satisfying.
2. Excessive materialism.	2. Same as above.
3. Lacks optimism and faith in your abilities as a man.	3. Demonstrate the process and study and counsel that you have exercised in coming to your conclusions and in setting the direction for yourself and the family.
Other Feminine Unbalanced Behaviors:	**Other Masculine Balancing Behaviors:**
1. Physically abusive to others.	1. Physical restraint and outside help if required.

Chapter 14:
Masculine-Feminine Balance of Power

"A man and a woman share equal power in a relationship at all times whether they recognize it or not. There are no victims and there are no villains; only two people wielding and directing their power." – Rakhem Seku

First, let me state that men and women share equal power in relationships at all times regardless of whether it is acknowledged or not. The masculine and feminine components exist equally in all interactions and they both have equal power to affect change in the relationship *(see the Yin/Yang picture below as a representation of this masculine and feminine balance)*. If there is any man out there who thinks he is "running" his relationship, he is in for trouble and a rude awakening because it's not true. Please do not buy into the patriarchal nonsense about men wearing the pants without the right context. Yes, a man's leadership role in relationships may be more visible and his actions more recognized, but that does not mean he has more power and influence.

There are multiple challenges when it comes to using our power in relationships, the first one being a proper understanding of what our power is, and second, how and when it should be used. From what I've seen, men do not understand women's power at all. This is, at the very least, inefficient in relation to building a solid relationship and future for one another, in addition to being down right dangerous in the worst case. Men should not feel too badly about not understanding women's power because women do not understand it themselves. This is apparent based on how some women apply themselves using a masculine approach to achieving success in life. I talk to numerous men who are having a rough time in their relationships. By that I mean their women are wearing them out emotionally and mentally on a day-to-day basis, and they are showing the signs of pain and defeat. The issue is not just that we are having a rough time, but more the fact that we don't even recognize it.

113

Diagram of the Yin and Yang in balance

Broadly stated, metaphysically a masculine power is physical, overt, and conscious, and a feminine power is mental, covert, and subconscious. What that means is that the masculine affects change in the world through overt physical conduct, which also can be viewed as varying degrees of conflict. As men, we achieve in life by going out and getting what we need and physically and openly influencing change. There is nothing covert about a masculine nature and activity. Can a man be covert? Sure, but what I am saying is that all men are born with a passion and desire to influence the world physically in a very real and explicit way. Men prefer and tend to choose overt actions because we want immediate credit and recognition for what we do. Again, let me say that I am referring to our inherent nature as men, as opposed to what we choose to do. This is important because it is the ignorance of our own nature that tends to cause challenges in our relationships, so we are educating ourselves here to empower ourselves to make the best choices.

An example of this would be with the most popular professional sport in America—football. Football is a game wherein your only objective is to subdue your opponent physically and run roughshod throughout their territory. It is a physical game in which all parts of the body can be used to get the job done, unlike soccer, tennis, or other sports in which rules greatly limit your physical movement. Tennis could be the number one sport if a player could hop over the net and whack their opponent in the kneecaps with their racket and then shove the ball down his throat to go up fifteen-love. Even soccer could compete for number one if the ball could be picked up with your hands or your opponent could be tackled before he scores. Rugby is popular in Europe because it is a physical game with groups of men on the field going at it, where on the other hand, it is not popular in America because the best athletes are in other sports. But trust me, if men with football player-type statures started playing rugby, the game would become increasingly popular. Just start putting guys on a rugby field who weigh 350 pounds, bench 500 pounds, and run a 4.5, 40-yard dash—now we're talking! But then again that would just lead us back to football because you would have to pad those guys up or expect 10-20 percent fatalities every year. Unfortunately, men have no real outlet to exercise the physical power within them outside of sports or the military.

"A man in his masculine nature will find that his core power is physical, overt, and conscious, whereas a woman in her feminine nature will find that her core power is mental, covert, and subconscious."

Of course, I am not saying that men do not have mental power and capabilities; I am saying our physical power is the primary force at work in his life. A man's mental abilities show up the most in his Monk and Leader character traits (as discussed in previous chapters). However, when you look at relationships and what tends to impact our women, we find it is our physicality and overt natures. Our masculine nature shows up in a number of other areas of responsibility in the relationship, especially with sex. Most women require that a man take control during love making, starting from its initiation; it is what keeps them moist, orgasmic, and fertile. I am not just talking a man's preference, but what's required to maintain a certain level of our masculine nature. Being in our physical and overt natures is what keeps us virile and potent as men and strengthens our leadership abilities. The fact that a number of men are not in their masculine natures has contributed to the rise in impotence and relationship issues in general.

So it has been asserted that a man's power is physical in nature with the understanding that he has mental capabilities as well. Next we need to clarify a woman's innate power. Quite simply, when we say that a woman's power is mental, it means that she can have and attract whatever she wants simply by thinking about it, essentially like magnets. By now we have all heard of the concept of the Law of Attraction, which basically states that whatever you really think, feel, and believe is what will manifest in your life. Women "own" the Law of Attraction; it is a feminine principle through and through. Can men use the Law of Attraction? Sure thing, but it is women who were bestowed with the essential and most powerful tools to use this law at birth. That is what we mean when we say women own the mental capabilities, which is the source of their power. To visualize something in her mind down to the minutest detail over a long period of time is a feminine principle.
Unfortunately, women use this power mostly when they are stressed or worried about the worst-case scenario of a situation; thus they are bringing the situation into existence, when instead they can also use the same power positively to counteract negative outcomes. This is the secret and key to life and is how we create our realities.

Women who are proficient at this skill have everything they need and are happy—it is guaranteed according to the Law of Attraction. Below is a break down of the formula:

> **Mental image + Perceived Benefit/Harm + Emotion = Manifested Reality**

You literally can take this formula to the bank!

The table below should add some clarity to the roles men and women have in relationships, and more specifically, the creative process that couples can use to bring about what they desire.

Masculine-Feminine Balance of Power Matrix

Masculine	Feminine
Direction Setting	**Vision/Strategy**
Sets direction, goals (long and short term), and objectives for the family or relationship. Answers the question, "What should we do?" The goals come from deep contemplative thinking around the subject at hand as well as research and counsel from qualified individuals in their fields of expertise.	Determines how (the plan) goals and objectives will be fulfilled. Responsible for maintaining the family's or relationship's faith in the original goal(s). Answers the question, "How do we get this done?" The how comes in the form of ideas and creative thinking along with a broad understanding of what is required to get the ideas moving.

Leadership	Devotion
Determines who will do what tasks to achieve the goals and objectives of the family or relationship and manages the process from start to finish. Answers the question, "Who is best qualified to execute the plan and where will the resources come from?" This is accomplished by being present and in touch with one's environment and everyone in it, as well as knowing their strengths, weaknesses, desires, passions, and requirements for making them successful in life.	The living, breathing representation of true commitment to the family or relationship and the outcome of any and all objectives. Answers the question, "Why should we pursue this goal?" This devotion is accomplished by having a vision of the final desired outcome of the family; including the achievement of all respective goals and objectives.
Self-Sacrifice (Soldiering)	**Worldly Sacrifice (Conservation)**
Ensures that the physical effort is put forth to protect the family, relationship, or end goal at all costs and ensures successful implementation of the goal, even in the face of personal harm or loss.	Ensures that the family's or relationship's health, well-being, survival, and prosperity are prioritized and accounted for before committing resources and effort to others.
Negotiation	**Love**
Sets the tone for all social	Sets the tone for all intimate

interaction and defines how the family or relationship and individuals will define themselves to others. Answers the question, "Who are we and how do we define ourselves?" This is done every time you discuss the family or relationship or when someone asks you how everyone is doing and is primarily done through verbal and written communication.	interaction and defines the look and feel of the family or relationship as a unit and for each individual. Determines etiquette for behavior also. Answers the question, "Who are we and how do we want to feel and present ourselves to others?" This is done any time you present yourself at home or in public and is all about how you look, act, and feel.

Chapter 15:
The Abuse of Power

"We are still in recovery." – Maya Greenejones

Now that we have a picture of men's and women's power, we need to identify the signs of its abuse. This is important because we need to hold ourselves and loved ones accountable for how we influence change in our lives. The good news for men is that it is easy to identify abuses in our power; that is part of the benefit of living in a male-oriented society. In addition to that, because it *is* men who recognize and respect masculine power and its potential abuse, many rules, laws, and social protocols are already in effect to deter men from abusing these powers.

Masculine power abuse is defined as: **any overt physical action performed outside of one's given realm of responsibility for the purpose of forcing another person to move or react against their will**. Physical action can be defined as: **any action that is perceptible by one or more of the five senses: touch, taste, smell, hearing, or sight** (which are all really the same sense experienced through different input channels or parts of the body). This gives us a broad definition for physical abuse, which is often inaccurately made synonymous to domestic violence. Some examples of physical abuse are:

- Using any part of your body (e.g., hands, arms, feet, teeth, or head) against another person's body hitting, strangling, grabbing, etc.
- Speaking loudly or forcibly such that the tone is harsh or offensive; it is not the words as much as the tone and raw sound that can be used as a symbol to precede physical violence.

Feminine power abuse is defined as: **any covert physical action (knife in the back) or mental action (visualization, wishing, and the like) performed outside of one's given realm of responsibility that forces another person to move or react against their**

will. A covert action can be defined as: **any action that does not affect one or more of the five senses (touch, taste, smell, hearing, or sight)**. This gives us a broad definition for mental abuse, which is never associated with domestic violence. Some examples of mental abuse are:

- Visualizing, wishing or thinking about physical outcomes that may cause harm to others
- Speaking in such a way that implies something may happen without being explicit or in many cases not saying anything at all. Here it's the specific word choice as opposed to the tone.

The implication of things to come was the worst for me. I remember having arguments with my wife and thinking I had gotten the best of her only to realize the joke was on me because I was too scared to go to sleep. It was an excruciating experience lying there in the dark wondering about all the possible negative things that could happen once I dozed off. Just tell me you're going to kick my ass rather than have me try and figure out what you're going to do myself. That is the kind of stuff that will turn you grey!

Abuse of Power in Relationships

The focus of this section is to clarify and also bring to light exactly how and why men and women tend to overuse and abuse their power in relationships. Because of our cultural influences, men are apt to define power in narrow terms usually oriented toward its masculine expression. When this occurs, we lose our ability to respect our partner and subsequently function appropriately with them. This happens more so when men do not understand how a woman's power and influence is manifesting in the relationship. But in defense of men, I have found very few women who understand their own power and how to use it to manifest happiness in their lives. This is why many women claim to be victims in their relationships, as opposed to equal participants.

Men and women bring equal power and influence to relationships. The notion that either a man or a woman has the upper hand in any relationship is based on social and cultural misconceptions, as opposed to an understanding of the universal laws that govern everything we do. For example, even in a situation in which it appears that a man has control over a woman in a relationship because he makes all the money, has all the skills, is more educated or what have you—it is an illusion that he has painted for himself. In fact, it is impossible for any one person to gain more than their fair share of control in a relationship, but ignorance of this fact sometimes leads people to try to gain control and influence the behavior of their partners. This is an abuse of power and it usually manifests itself in one of two forms—either physical or mental.

We defined feminine and masculine abuses of power earlier, so now let's define physical and mental abuse. Simply put, physical abuse is defined as: **an attempt to control the will (choices) of another person through deformation of their body**. On the other hand, mental abuse: **is the attempt to control the will (choices) of another person through the deformation of their mind**. Both forms, physical and mental, are equally damaging to the persons they are carried out upon, but their influences manifest themselves in very different ways.

But why attempt to influence the choices that our mates make, or why force someone to view the world as we do?

123

The answer to both questions is having a fear of the unknown and a lack of respect for others.

Part of the issue is thinking that the other person is not considering our point of view, which is a deeper issue than that person not taking the time to fully appreciate us as a person. If you are in a relationship with someone who doesn't appreciate you then maybe you should seek outside help. Maybe they don't appreciate you because they don't know how, in which case patience, time, and consistent work to understand the person better would be beneficial. If they don't appreciate you because they don't respect you then it's a different problem entirely. Either way, however, forcing someone to listen to you or forcing them to do something against their will whether through physical or mental influence is not the answer. Even forcing someone to listen to your point of view is not really justifiable when you think about it. Remember, everything in life is about choice. Maybe the issue is fear of the unknown. Sometimes it can be unbearable to think what may happen if things don't go the way we think they should or if things don't get done the way we think they ought too. So, we do everything in our power to ensure they do go the way we want them to, including forcing others to fall in line.

The fear also comes from us losing a belief in ourselves resulting in losing a belief in our value as human beings. If we are wrong, then we must be worthless, right? If we do not contribute our views to the world, and subsequently the world doesn't embrace them, then all is for naught. Why even be here? So as a result, we hold on to our beliefs for fear of becoming obsolete and we fight for dear life to be heard. As a consultant, I had the opportunity to meet and work with a number of dynamic women. One young lady in particular would talk to me about her relationship woes on a regular basis. She would always say, "I will be heard" when referring to the men in her life. Meaning, they were going to hear her opinion, respect it, and in most cases implement it as stated. My wife used to say something similar whenever we would have our joking disagreements. She would say, "I gets what I wants," then laugh it off. But she meant that; believe me.

One Last Word on Domestic Violence

The core of domestic violence is usually caused by both men and women's ignorance of their essential natures. The bottom line is most people just do not know who they are or what they bring to the table in a relationship. As a result, they conduct themselves in a dysfunctional manner inside of dysfunctional relationships, usually pointing the finger at each other without acknowledging their own role as the primary source of their problems. Speaking from experience, my wife and I have been through a lot, but we have learned that the issue is *us* equally at all times. This is how we have managed to stay together for so many years and be effective relationship coaches to others.

When most people refer to domestic violence, they are referring to physical abuse when one person uses excessive physical force to impose their will upon another. Men tend to be the ones to abuse their physical power in relationships because that is one of their primary power sources—the ability to change physically one's environment through direct confrontation. No one should ever use his or her power to impose their will on others, but unfortunately, this is a part of human nature we are meant to evolve past as we come into adulthood. We have all been in power positions at some point in our lives and have had to make choices on how to use that power responsibly. Many times we succeed; yet, still many

125

times we fail. When we fail we end up hurting others, especially those we love.

As stated previously, when we speak of relationships, the popular belief is that men somehow hold all the power in a relationship, when this is not the case. In any relationship, the power is always shared equally by those who participate in it according to the laws of physics, biology, and chemistry, wherein two objects that share the same environment are given the same amount of power, will, and expression. There are no examples in life where one object/entity holds more power than its counterpart, although sometimes it may appear that way. Unfortunately, living in a traditionally and historically male-oriented society, women's power, at the very least, is not understood and, more often than not, is ignored or actively suppressed (it's actually impossible to suppress someone's power, including feminine power; however, historically attempts have been made nonetheless).

I emphasize this point because the issues that men have are: 1) thinking that they are somehow in control of things (in other words, not understanding themselves); and 2) not understanding their partners and women in general. As a result, men open themselves up to mental or emotional abuse, which causes them to remove themselves mentally and emotionally from the relationship. This is why men retreat, so to speak, when things get rough in relationships to video games, sports shows, quiet parts of the house, or solace in other women. Our society has incorrectly taught us to hold in our feelings and attempt to deal with mental and emotional pressures without giving us the proper tools to successfully process these pressures; thus, we often find ourselves in a no-win situation. I recall as a child witnessing physical violence in adult relationships and marriage and being very clear what physical abuse looked like and how it impacted people, but I never understood mental abuse until much later in life. As men you need to know that it is all right to admit you are having trouble handling the mental pressures of your relationships.

I believe that we are all 100% responsible for our success and failures in life. In relationships (assuming two people) each person is 50% responsible for all successes and failures in that relationship; whether it be business, personal, or intimate in nature, relationships take real work and sincere effort to have any chance for success. It is easy to point the finger at other people as the source of our problems, but there is no growth in that approach.

<u>Signs of Mental and Emotional Abuse</u>

For men who recognize they are starting to retreat mentally from their relationship, they need to get help right away. This is a sign of not being able to handle what is going on in their relationship. Retreating is a natural response to pain. When we are in danger or experiencing pain, our first response is to find a more nurturing and peaceful environment. When men find themselves mentally retreating from their mates, it is a sign they need support and understanding to help them along. If they cannot find knowledgeable people to help them, they should leave the situation and the environment if necessary until help is found. Otherwise, the symptoms of their mental and emotional challenges will become the primary issue in the relationship, as opposed to the issues of incompatibility of natures that caused the retreat in the first place. The symptoms to look for are:

1.   Being annoyed at your mate (i.e. she is getting on your nerves)
2.   Ignoring her or acting in a passive-aggressive fashion when she is attempting to reach out to you

3.   Not taking care of home duties as a passive-aggressive move to hurt her and regain your power in the relationship
4.   Arguing with her
5.   Visualizing yourself with other women or in a different situation as an attempt to escape your current reality
6.   Dating other women in an attempt to gain the respect and love you feel you are not getting at home.

These are just a few symptoms, but I am sure you get the message. Do not attempt to be clever and say you are cool if you are not; nothing is gained in doing that. If your thoughts are that you can change the relationship dynamic around, you are correct, but not without taking 100% responsibility for your actions, which includes your choice to be with your partner. After all, the concepts in this book are based on empowerment, which means you have the power to do, say, or be whatever is required for success. A helpful prerequisite will be to understand why you have attracted this person into your life and what the lesson is; in other words, what deficiency is this person exposing within you that you need to work on? Refer back to the information in Chapter 5 on "reflection" — understanding how everyone in our lives is our reflection.

Women who see these signs in their men also need to get help immediately from a trusted advisor or counselor or remove themselves from the situation right away. They too can probably change the relationship dynamic, but not without the proper guidance and direction. In addition to receiving the proper guidance, removing the victim and guilt mentalities that women commonly associate with abuse is important so they can take complete responsibility and accountability for their lives. In the case of both men and women, if we view ourselves as a victim, we should not attempt to change anything because victims have no power to change, and if we chose to stay in the relationship when these signs are apparent, we immediately become a contributor to all that follows.

A final note is you need to seek help immediately or hopefully before you enter into a relationship if you fit any of the following criteria:

1. You have witnessed physical or mental/emotional abuse as a child or at any time in your life
2. You do not believe that both you and your partner contribute equally to the success and failure of the relationship
3. You do not believe you are 100% responsible for your life.

Chapter 16:
Healing Women Through Sex and Intimacy

"Bouncing down the walls of inhibition, evaporating all of my fears, baptizing me into complete submission, dissolving my condition with his tears. It's just like the water, I ain't felt this way in years...drowning me I find my insides sailing, drinking in the mainstream of his mind, filling up the cup of my emotions, spilling over into all I do, if only I could get lost in his ocean, surviving on the thought of loving you." – Lauryn Hill, Water

Kirikou: So... the Sorceress did not take the water away from the village, she did not eat the men, she prefers to eat yams... next you are going to say she's innocent and she loves everybody!
Kirikou's Grandfather: No, no. She dislikes children, she despises women, and she hates all men!
Kirikou: But why?
Kirikou's Grandfather: Because she is in pain!
– from the movie Kirikou and the Sorceress by Michael Ocelot

My wife wanted to have sex way more than I did. She was an every day, two-times-per-day type of woman and not at all unique in that regard. My college girlfriend was the same way. She wanted to have sex all the time, which was understandable because of the strong love that we felt for one another as well as her wanting to please me in the relationship. I remember a few times trying to sneak into my dorm room at night after studying late and get into bed hoping not to wake her up, but it rarely worked. My roommate also was experiencing the same thing with his girlfriend. One day he came to me in one of our rare moments alone together in our room and confided in me about his experiences with his girlfriend.

Neither of us had the solution or really understood the problem, but I think we were both relieved to hear we were not the only one having the issue. During the later teenage years a male's ego is super fragile. We are still experimenting with sex and learning the basics, and at the same time in serious competition with our peers to be with the highest number of the finest women possible, and added to that are the stresses of the variables associated with:

1. The size (length and width) of our penis
2. How often we have sex
3. How long we can penetrate and have rigorous intercourse with a woman before having an ejaculation
4. The level of beauty of the women we can attract
5. The number of women we can attract
6. How many orgasms the women we have sex with has (later in life)
7. Firmness of our penis (later in life).

As you can see 2 and 3 were at risk here because we were having a bit of trouble keeping up with our girlfriends. However, the risk for the male ego goes deeper than that, because if a woman is not pleased with you in any aspect of your relationship, then she may communicate to other women the true status, in her mind, of 1, 2, 3, 6, and 7, which is a man's worse nightmare—an angry woman dogging his penis.

As a man you just cannot go out like that or else it will ruin your reputation with the women, and yes, it was a real possibility that your penis could get trashed; whether it is true or not.

My girlfriend and I eventually broke up for a number of reasons, but I think partly because I was overwhelmed a bit from being in my first real relationship. I took a break from dating and started up again a number of months later. This lasted about a year and a half, but the difference was I was dating numerous women and having sex every night again. At any one time I may have had six solid girlfriends with whom I would have sex with at least once per week plus the additional women I would meet at the club, or on campus, or wherever. The point is I was having a lot of sex, but the tired factor did not weigh in the same; I was tired, but still pretty energized to do my thing. This is an important fact because many men find themselves drawn to and energized by a variety of women, but we need to understand why we are attracted to women in this way and what to do with that attraction. Men's sexual attraction to women has more to do with our desire to heal and rebalance women through sex and thus feel the power resulting from that healing. What I realized much later in my life was that I was doing more than having sex with these women; I was intimate with them and providing them healing in the process. How did I know I was healing women during sex? The primary ways I knew were:

(1) I was only intimate with women after I made a mental and emotional connection with them, which signaled our

intimacy was about us rather than me. This wasn't so much a spoken connection, but one they could feel through my actions and intention.

(2) I was in a "giver" mode during sex and prioritized her fulfillment, pleasure, and well-being first.

When men heal women they heal themselves and in turn are also energized during the process.

A Face-Value Discussion on Sex

As a relationships coach and someone who practices Tantra, it is safe to say that over eighty percent of my female clients want sex all the time, and in many cases, these same women wanted sex more than their man. The women who have low libidos oftentimes are suppressing their desire to have sex caused by traumatic experiences from their past. Let's provide a straightforward explanation for women's sex drive.

Women internalize everything that happens around them. As part of the internalization process, they hold onto those feelings whether good or bad and generally do not let them go. The truth is they cannot let them go, at least not without some effective tools like Tantra or meditation. Imagine having a painful experience or a stressful day and never letting it go, but instead storing that stress and pain in your mind's memory and cells of your body. You can only do that for so long before something has to give. Either you have a mechanism for releasing those experiences bringing you back into balance, or you do not. Imagine if you do not know that you are holding on to this stress, but feel something is wrong and need an energetic release. This is what many women go through on a daily basis, and accordingly, they do need a release, but I would prefer to call it a healing or rebalancing of their energies because that is the result of releasing the stress.

Both men and women have naturally secreting hormones that generate the desire for sex. Men secrete testosterone and women secrete estrogen. Both of these hormones move men and women into their masculine and feminine modalities causing us to seek our complementary energetic partner. The bottom line is that women greatly appreciate intimacy in the form of closeness and touching and the touching provides physical and emotional healing.

Sex and Intimacy

The topic of sex and intimacy is a whole separate text in itself, but we need to mention it because they are critical components in our relationships and our emotional being. In this section we will come to an understanding on sex and intimacy and learn a few basic techniques to help us be successful sexually with our partners and also be fulfilled as men.

First, let's be clear that sex, or the act of having sex, and intimacy are two completely different things. Sex is an act of receiving, and intimacy is an act of giving. For the sake of this work, let's define sex.

> **Sex is an act of creation (not just babies) engaged in by individuals for the purpose of changing a current reality into a newly desired reality.**

The definition of intimacy is as follows...

Intimacy is an act of activation engaged in by individuals for the purpose of increasing one's electromagnetic field; therefore, rebalancing one's physical, mental, emotional, and spiritual body.

In plain English, sex is an act of creation. We engage in it to create babies, pleasure for ourselves, or for those who understand metaphysics; whatever you want. Generally, we can tell when we are about to engage in sex because the act is preceded with thoughts like, "I'm about to get a piece," or, "I really need some right now," or, "I'm horny." When you are in that mode, your whole intention is clear—the sexual experience you're about to engage in is about you. It is not that the women you are with will not also get pleasure from the act, but you want to be clear on your intention. Sex is fun, pleasurable, and necessary, so the fact that we are saying it is a receiving act does not make it bad.

This is important because if we look at sex as a creative act wherein we can literally change our reality to whatever we want it to be, whether we intend to make that change or not, it influences how we approach the act itself, including: who we choose to have sex with, what we tell our children about it and when we tell them, and the importance of being selfless, yet very intentional, during sex. Sexual intercourse is one of the most powerful tools that couples have to influence their lives and shape their relationship and it should not be taken lightly.

Intimacy is all about energizing and healing others. It lacks the selfishness we find in the sexual act and requires that we be physically and emotionally present with our partners at all times. It is an act of giving unselfishly without expecting anything in return. There are endless ways to be intimate with your partner; your creativity is the only limiting factor.

As men we should actively engage in intimacy with our mates at least a few times per week. In other words, we should take anywhere from two to four hours and provide pleasure to them just the way they want it. How do we know what they want? Well you better know, or like my calculus teacher used to say when we did not know how to approach a calculus problem, "You'll be sleeping in the streets." He was basically saying doing nothing is not an option. If you do not know what your mate desires, ask her. Ask something like, "If you could have a night with me and I provide you whatever kind of pleasure and intimacy you desire, what would it be?" After you know what she desires, *you need to give it to her*. Make all the plans and arrangements required to set aside the time to do it. I cannot tell you how much your relationship will improve if you do this.

Some examples of intimacy include:

- Gently touching any part of her body
- Massages
- Kissing any part of her body
- Providing a bath and washing her
- Tantric energy work (explained in more detail in my forthcoming book)
- Reading poetry to her
- Gently making love to her.

These are just some forms of intimacy; the important thing to remember is that it is her time.

Intimacy is something we should engage in with our children as well; it is very important for men to be in physical contact with their sons and daughters. My wife read somewhere that children require twelve intimate contacts per day to avoid insanity. It can be something as simple as a piggyback ride, wrestling, a hug, or holding them while you take a nap. Any way you choose to do it is fine, but the point is that it should be an intentional act for the purpose of energizing and healing those you love. Our daughters depend upon receiving intimacy from their fathers and other males in their family circle as their first training before interacting sexually and intimately with a man. She needs to learn about the hardness and firmness of a man's touch and persona in its proper perspective. Men are hard and firm, but also protective and reassuring. This experience at a young age will help our daughters discern the real men from those without the proper training or those with ill intent.

It is safe to say that in today's world, many young women do not know what to look for in a man. How do they separate a real man from one who seeks only to take from them? How do they as women attract these types of men into their reality? How can you attract something and recognize it if you have no idea what it is, how it feels, or what it looks like? On top of that, once you find this individual, you wouldn't recognize him anyway. I cannot tell you how many women have found the man of their dreams only to let him go because they couldn't recognize what they had. From a man's standpoint, do not feel bad about losing a woman you want to be with, because she may have not been the right one for you in the first place. The women we are externally attracted to are rarely the ones we need in our lives over the long term.

When I met my wife, I already knew what kind of woman I was looking for. I had a vision of her general shape and demeanor a few weeks prior to meeting her. The funny thing is that I ended up meeting her girlfriend who had almost the same exact qualities and I tried to talk to her first. When Maya never called me back I was a bit disappointed, but not disheartened because I was confident I would meet the right one soon. A few weeks later, I met my wife on a blind date, and I was not surprised that she looked just like Maya—same height, same body shape, lips, hips, everything.

The point here is that you will attract the one that is meant for you and the one that matches your vibration at that time. When I say vibration I am referring to one's current desire and focus at any particular time in life. I remember when I was ready to get married and settle down I met Kenya; she was in the same place, too. There were other women I was interested in at the time, but we just never came together. The bottom line is those other women and I were not on the same vibration, meaning we were essentially looking for different things in a relationship.

Modern culture has reduced sex to an act of selfish pleasure, self-gratification, and entertainment, while also stigmatizing it as "dirty.". The effects of viewing sex in this way have been devastating and have wreaked havoc on our children and our relationships. It is time to upgrade our understanding of sex and intimacy and use it in ways that benefit our relationships.

Bringing Women to Orgasm

Let me make some definitive statements here so that we are clear about a woman and her orgasmic potential during sex. It is a man's responsibility to bring a woman to orgasm during sex, not hers. Men intuitively know this fact, which is why they are so sensitive about it after sex. But let's clarify that statement so we can all be on the same page. Women are naturally orgasmic; being orgasmic is their birthright. A man's role is to provide security, reassurance, and be physically and emotionally present with her throughout the process so she can experience her own femininity to its highest potential. This is different from her masturbating, which involves any form of manipulating her own body or her partner's body. A man is not doing his job if the woman is manipulating her body during the sexual act to achieve clitoral orgasms. Women should have multiple full-body, vaginal, and clitoral orgasms during *any* sexual encounter with a man. A healthy orgasm for a woman should also include her ejaculating fluid during the orgasm although it's not required for a fulfilling sexual experience. Women should give themselves completely to the man during sex and failure to do so leads to failure of the man to bring trust and security to her. Any woman will relax and let the man take over during sex (or any situation for that matter) if she trusts his leadership. True, she may have some hang ups around trusting and having faith, but it's your job as a man to facilitate the healing required to fix those issues. Her trust and faith issues also points to our inability as men to be in one or more of the four masculine character traits discussed earlier in this book.

Chapter 17:
Momma

"...ain't a woman alive that can take my momma's place"
– Tupac Shakur

The most important lessons a boy learns from his mother is how a woman is supposed to function—period. How can you relate to women or identify a woman for a wife if you have never seen one before? It would almost be laughable if it were not so serious how people go about choosing a mate. What are the criteria? How do you choose which woman you will spend the rest of your life with? Do you choose her by how she looks, if she can cook, how good she is in bed, the number of college degrees she has, how much money she makes, or maybe, if she tends to agree with you most of the time? If so, I see trouble on the horizon my friend. If the above factors held any real weight, we would see a much higher happiness rate in relationships because many people choose their partners based on one or more of these factors.

I stated earlier in the book that many men are angry at their mothers because they subconsciously blame them for the failures of the relationship between them and their fathers regardless of the reason. Children don't really care about who is wrong or right because intuitively they know it doesn't matter. So why are men angry at their mothers? It is because they are left with no example of what to look for in a woman. Yes, he can observe the superficial things like cooking, being patient with siblings, teaching children the basics, working hard, and the list could go on. But this list pales in comparison to not learning how a woman is supposed to treat a man and function in a relationship.

Times have changed so much over the decades that many of the traditional roles men and women play are now blurred; however, what remains essential for a healthy relationship is our consciousness as men and women. Without that you have insanity in the house, no exaggeration. Today I can look back more objectively at examples of how I was functioning in my relationships and see that I was out of my role in many cases.

Of course, it is obvious that men also blame their fathers for the issues they see in their relationships. We are not saying men are putting all the blame on their mothers. The father's faults are more straightforward, like him leaving instead of hanging in there and figuring things out, or losing his cool on a regular basis when he could have tried to maintain a level head. On a subconscious level, an even bigger issue is not knowing how to "tame his inner woman" or how to heal his wife not having been given the proper tools to do so. Without an initiation into manhood, he is now stuck in boy mode or, worse than that, woman mode with no hopes of taming his inner woman. Let's face it, it's not fair to expect women to show up unscathed from their life adventures before meeting you. So understanding how to heal women is essential, but who is going to teach you about women let alone tell you what dangers lie ahead in the absence of a father or male figure?

How do you know if you have anger or unresolved issues with your mother? Ask yourself if you primarily take from women or give to them. Do you display behavior that reflects a general disdain, disrespect, or anger towards women? If your intention is to give to them all that you have to offer for the purpose of seeing them happy, then you do not have mother anger. But if you look to be nurtured primarily by women and receive love, time, and attention from them, you have mother anger or, at the very least, have not received everything you needed from her as a child.

If you determine you have some anger towards your mother there are definite ways to deal with it. First, is forgiving yourself for any perceived transgressions or relationship failures you have had in life. We have to stop the cycle of blaming ourselves or anyone else for our perceived shortcomings in relationships and realize we are a work-in-progress. Second, we need to forgive our mother's and father's for not giving us what we think we needed from them to be successful in life. In all cases, our parents do the best they can in raising and loving us even when it seems they haven't tried or have fallen substantially short. I know that may be tough to accept sometimes, but it's true. We have to remember that they are dealing with their own traumas and have been through numerous life challenges that have greatly impacted their ability to support us completely. Third, we need to forgive the women in our past relationships. This is important because we as men tend to build up resentment towards women for not giving us what we think we need from them, but we need to realize that often times we tend to put a heavier burden on them than they can realistically handle. In addition, they are dealing with their own traumas and attempting to heal and move forward in their lives. Forth, we need to know, that we are capable of having healthy lives and relationships regardless of our past experiences. We always have the power to do, become, and create what we want out of life.

Chapter 18:
Women Want to be Vulnerable

"The fact is we need you." – Jill Scott

The truth is many women want to be vulnerable and tell men the truth of how they need them and want them in their lives. Trust me, many women have very specific needs that require a man's touch whether they want to admit it or not. They want men to save them and take responsibility for their physical and emotional well - being. More than they care to admit, these women want to be secured, protected, and loved.

The bottom line is that many women will not admit they have any needs at all from a man other than sex and for him to provide some support here and there. You should ignore that message because it is not the whole story. So what do you do when women refuse to open up to you and tell you what they need? You give them what they need anyway. It is not about them telling you what they need because intuitively you already know what you should do; it is more about actually providing it. You earn their trust through your actions over the long term; eventually you will begin to see them opening up to you slowly over time. Bringing forth the four masculine principles as presented in this book is the way to go and does not require them to change their behavior in any way.

Made in the USA
Lexington, KY
27 January 2012